SURFER
MAGAZINE

SURFRIDERS

IN SEARCH OF THE PERFECT WAVE

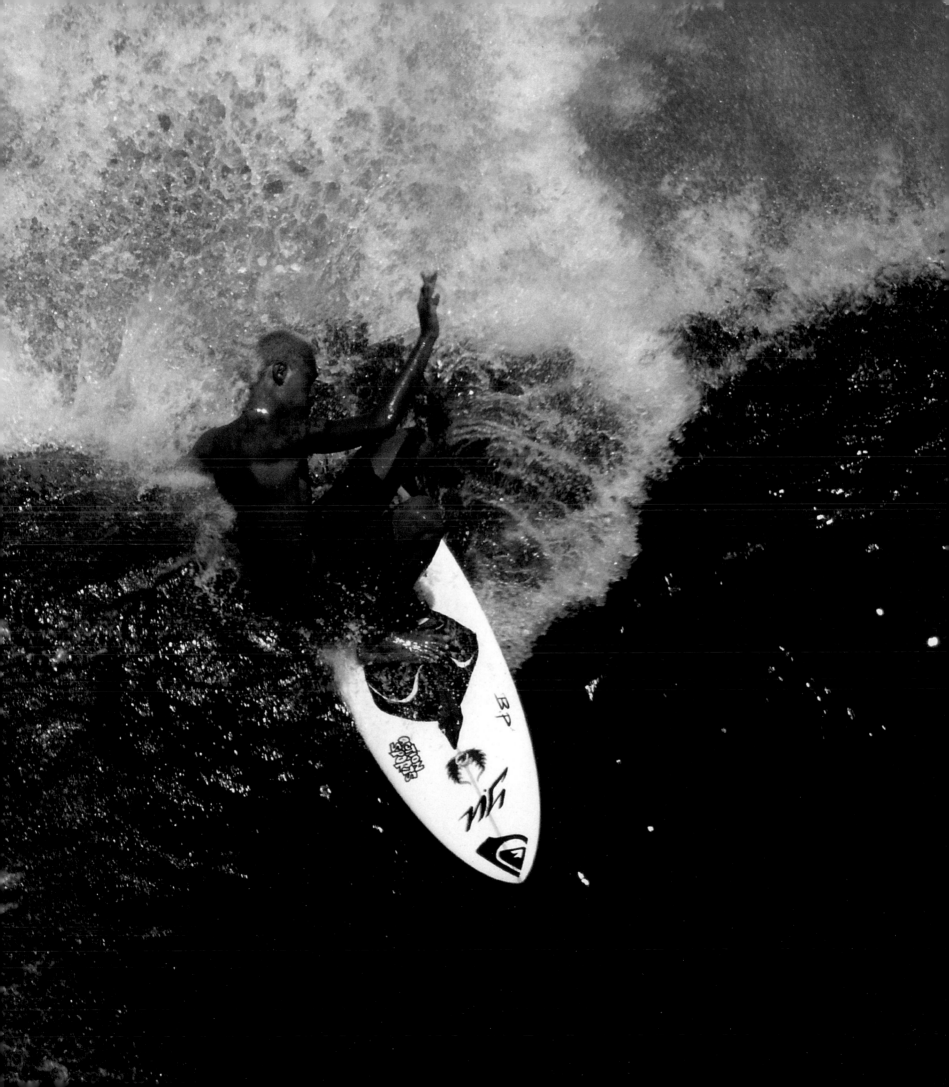

SURFER MAGAZINE

SURF RIDERS

IN SEARCH OF THE PERFECT WAVE

MATT WARSHAW

FOREWORD BY TOM CARROLL INTRODUCTION BY STEVE HAWK

CollinsPublishers

A Division of HarperCollinsPublishers

SurfRiders was conceived and produced by Tehabi Books, Del Mar, California. Nancy Cash–*Managing Editor;* Andy Lewis–*Art Director;* Sam Lewis–*Art Director;* Tom Lewis–*Editorial and Design Director;* Sharon Lewis–*Controller;* Chris Capen–*President.* Additional support for *SurfRiders* was also provided by Rob Gilley–*Photo Editor;* Steve Pezman–*Editorial Consultant;* Susan Wels–*Copy Editor;* and Lisa Eilertson–*Proofreader.*

HarperCollins books may be purchased for educational, business, or sales promotional use. For information please write: Special Markets Department, HarperCollins Publishers, Inc., 10 East 53rd Street, New York, NY 10022.

For corporate customized editions, please contact: Chris Capen, Tehabi Books, 1201 Camino Del Mar, Suite 100, Del Mar, California, 92014; 619/481-7600.

For surf shop and surf industry sales worldwide, please contact *Surfer Magazine,* P.O. Box 1028, Dana Point, CA 92629 800/854-4040.

Tehabi Books, in association with The Basic Foundation, a not-for-profit organization whose primary mission is reforestation, will facilitate the planting of two trees for every one tree used in the manufacture of this book.

Library of Congress Cataloging-in-Publication Data
　　Warshaw, Matt, 1960-
　　　　SurfRiders: in search of the perfect wave / Matt Warshaw.
　　　　　　p.　　cm.
　　　　"Conceived and produced by Tehabi Books"--T.p. verso.
　　　　Includes bibliographical references (p.)
　　　　ISBN 0-00-649179-0 (pbk. : alk. paper)
　　　　1. Surfing—History. 2. Surfing—pictorial works. I. Title.
　　GV840.S8W346　1997
　　797.3'2--dc21　　　　　　　　　　　　　　96-46803
　　　　　　　　　　　　　　　　　　　　　　　CIP

99 00 / 10 9 8 7 6 5 4

This edition is printed on acid-free paper that meets the American National Standards Institute Z39.48 Standard.
Printed in China

Photo Captions:
front cover: Kahea Hart, Rocky Point; back cover: Cloudbreak, Fiji; page 1: Darrick Doerner, Jaws; pages 2-3: Rezal Tanjung, Rocky Point; pages 4-5: Mike Parsons, Todos Santos; page 6: Matt Archbold, Off the Wall; pages 8-9: Cloudbreak, Fiji.

CONTENTS

FOREWORD
by Tom Carroll

The sky is orange and crimson, but the sun hasn't yet come over the horizon. Any moment now it will appear. A warm sense of well-being floods through me. For 27 years now, the sunlight has been a companion during my early-morning presurfing ritual.

At age 7, I didn't linger at dawn the way I sometimes do today—although I was becoming aware of the range of nature's subtleties that surfers learn. I figured out, for example, that if the tips of the two poplar trees in our backyard were leaning slightly toward the beach, it meant that the wind was blowing offshore. And I learned that a deep, muffled rumble meant big waves. Of course, some winter mornings would fool me. I'd wake up to hear one loud crack! after another, only to discover, after a mad rush to the beach, that the noise was caused by tiny waves breaking onto an inshore sandbar, amplified somehow in the cold air.

From the start, my companions and I saw surfing as an invitation to explore. After we'd covered every inch of our local beach, we'd plan a jaunt around the nearby rocky headland to the next beach over. Maybe there were better waves there. And what about the beach up around the next headland? We'd find out soon enough.

And, of course, there were competitive urges. I'll never forget this one kid running up to me in the school playground and boasting about "Crolley," his good mate: "Hey, Tommy! Did you hear? Crolley did a vertical reentry on an overhead wave yesterday!" Well, I knew Crolley was a good surfer, but—a vertical reentry on an overhead wave?! Awesome. I had to try it. And then I had to try it on a *bigger* wave. Competition would be an important aspect of my surfing life for years and years. Contests were also part of the adventure, putting me in touch with a variety of cultures around the world.

Today, at 35, I continue to be fascinated by the ocean. Its curves and colors have shaped my personal aesthetic. Its perpetual and unknowable changes appeal to my sense of curiosity.

Now the morning sun is slanting through the yard. From my window I can see a new 5-foot swell. The sandbar is just right. The wind is calm. But the tide isn't quite there yet, so I'll take some time waxing up a new board. What a feeling. There never was, and never will be, one quite like it. 🏄

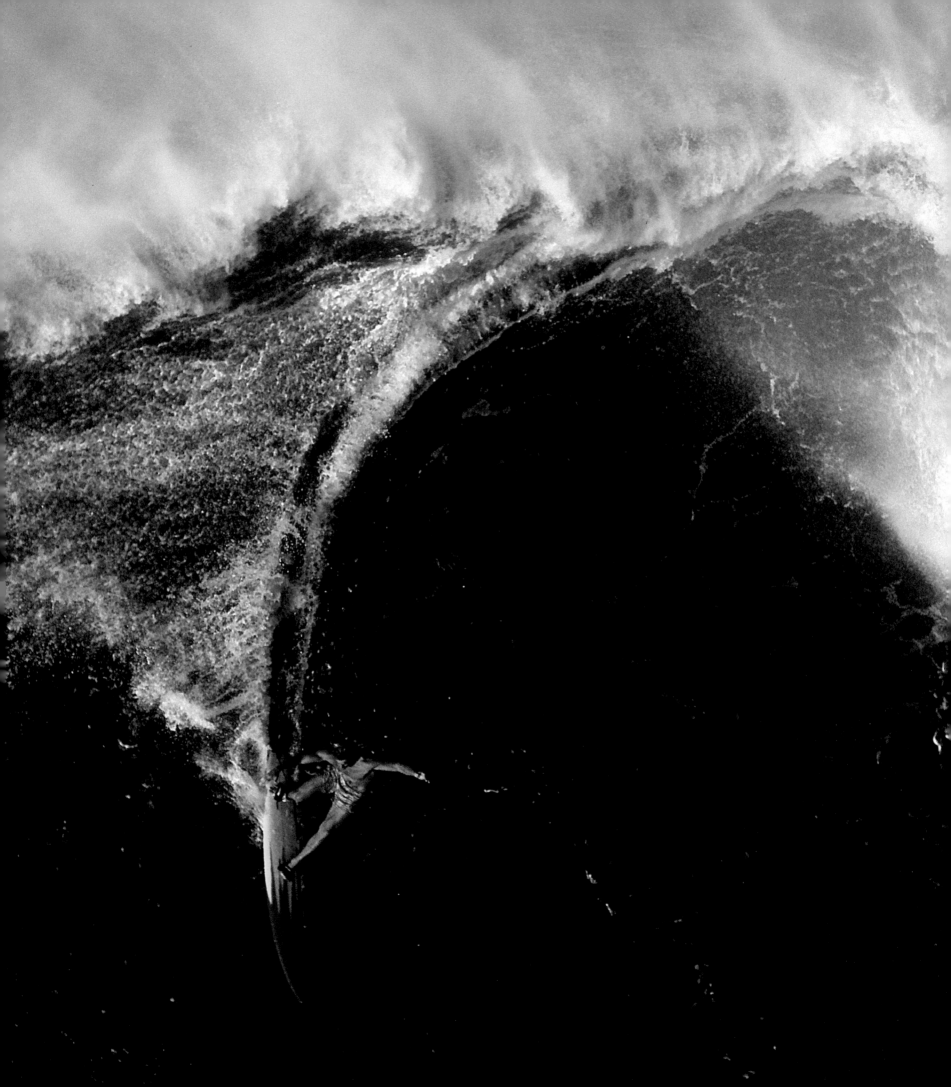

INTRODUCTION
by Steve Hawk

At the end of this book, Matt Warshaw argues that the sport of surfing is finally starting to earn—and I do mean *earn*—some of the respect its practitioners believe it has long deserved. As evidence of this newly burnished reputation, Warshaw notes the recent appearance of several documentaries and published works that have granted surfing "a weight and standing unimaginable during the era of Frankie and Annette." Ironically, he had to omit the book that best illustrates his point: this one.

Scores of books have been published about surfing over the past 50 years. The vast majority fall into one of three categories: coffee table books with stunning photos and mindless text; dry, predictable histories by barefoot bores; and rosy autobiographies by "legends" trying to claim a small parcel of immortality. The broad ones tend to be bad, the good ones arcane.

But here, Warshaw has taken a new approach, aiming his diamond-tipped research tools at six pivotal moments in the history of modern surfing. Each of these moments is compelling in its own right—from the day Duke Kahanamoku introduced the sport to Australia in 1914 to the day 80 years later when Laird Hamilton and his friends from Maui used WaveRunners to tow each other into the biggest waves ever ridden. More importantly, Warshaw skillfully pulls back the curtain on each anecdote to reveal larger, more provocative themes—how Duke helped resuscitate the majestic sport of his ancestors, then spent his last years neglected and impoverished. Or how the tow-in crew didn't simply ride bigger waves, but took a jackhammer to the sport's foundation. As Warshaw puts it:

> On a gut level, using the boat to tow them meant these guys *were* cheating. *On another level, they were stretching or breaking esthetic laws. Surfers regularly find peace, beauty, solitude, even God, in the ocean. Nonmechanization is considered to be a precondition to such feelings of calm and equanimity. Hamilton and his friends, as many saw it, had done nothing less than run a Harley through the hanging gardens.*

You might notice something else in the preceding excerpt: the boy can write. As the editor of *Surfer Magazine*, it has been my pleasure to edit many of Matt's articles, and I have come to regard him not only as surfing's most knowledgeable historian, but also as one of its best wordsmiths. He loves the craft of writing almost as much as he loves a good tube ride. Each passion is vividly apparent throughout these pages.

In addition to Warshaw's fine journalism, *SurfRiders* benefits from its focus on the world's most photogenic sport. Much credit is due here to Rob Gilley, who compiled the images in this book. Gilley has long been known as a talented surf photographer, but it turns out he's a thoughtful and persistent photo editor as well.

One last thing about *SurfRiders:* it dances with style on that tightrope stretched between readers who surf and readers who don't. I've read a lot about surfing over the past 25 years—a lot—and yet every few paragraphs here I found a new fact, discovered a new anecdote, or was provoked to think in some new way about the sport that defines my life. At the same time, nothing in these six chapters feels esoteric. Warshaw uses slang sparingly, and studiously avoids that vast library of surf clichés. I assume you know, or at least want to know, something about surfing to have picked up this book in the first place. If so, prepare yourself for a long and satisfying ride through new waters.

Chris Menzie rides the tube at Big Rock, in San Diego County. Although tube-riding has long been thought of as surfing's most treasured moment, it has always resisted easy description. Famous surfers were asked to put the feeling into words in 1970. A few responses: "I feel as a babe in the womb." "At peace with the whole world." "A feeling of weightlessness and nothingness." "Like I'm locked in a closet with Raquel Welch."

MORNING AT FRESHWATER

DUKE KAHANAMOKU
INTRODUCES SURFING TO AUSTRALIA

Duke Kahanamoku worked in the clear heat at Freshwater Beach, Australia, adz in hand, wood chips scattered around his bare ankles, with a sun-dried length of sugar pine suspended horizontally before him at waist level. The 24-year-old stopped and for a few moments let his eyes move across the rough planes of the unfinished surfboard. The year was 1914. Kahanamoku was two weeks through his first visit to Australia, which meant he'd acclimated in general but nonetheless had to pause often to assess local customs, methods, and materials. The regional wood, for example, was different from that found in the Honolulu lumber yards, so the board under construction was made of medium-density sugar pine, rather than Kahanamoku's preferred stock of dense Hawaiian koa—an obstacle likely met with a thoughtful look and a little shrug of resignation.

The developing board looked rudimentary even by early 20th-century standards: squared-off at the tail, sides gradually flared to a spot about three-quarters forward, then pulled together into a point. Kahanamoku would make dozens of notably sleek and streamlined boards in years to come, but this one looked like a 9-foot crayon. A measure of thought went into the design, however, as Kahanamoku, experimenting, chiseled out a concave section in the front of the hull. The waves at Freshwater seemed to be of average height and power, but the ocean surface itself looked to be of a rougher texture than that found in Waikiki, and he thought the concave feature would lend a stabilizing effect to his new board.

Kahanamoku's sugar-pine contrivance was actually the second authentic full-length surfboard in Australia. Charles Paterson of Manly, a local businessman and politician, had shipped a board in from Hawaii two years earlier, but he and a few bodysurfing friends were at a complete loss when they dragged it into the shorebreak for a test ride. The redwood import had been given a quiet and ignominious second life in the Paterson home as an ironing board.

Paterson, a swimmer, had never met Kahanamoku, but he knew of him and had been light-headed with anticipation since Kahanamoku's arrival in Australia. Sportsmen everywhere recognized the pure-blooded Hawaiian not just as the fastest swimmer alive and an Olympic gold-medal winner but as an international celebrity. Many also knew him as the world's greatest exemplar of the newly revived sport of

Duke Kahanamoku (previous spread) in Australia with Freshwater Beach admirers on December 23, 1914. Kahanamoku began surfing in 1898, when the ancient Hawaiian sport was thought of as a lost art. In the mid-1960s, he recalled his early board-riding experiences: "I was about 8 years old, when I started here at Waikiki Beach. That was a long time ago. We had nobody here to teach us how to ride these waves. We had to learn ourselves." (Opposite page) Kahanamoku's handmade sugar-pine surfboard is delivered to the beach at Freshwater.

surfing—or "board-shooting," as the Australian press called it. Kahanamoku, whose self-confidence was faulty at best, tended to view himself as little more than a gypsy son of Waikiki.

Australia had put him into a state of deep ambivalence, and his perpetually quiet manner now ranged from smiling and nonchalant to stoic and withdrawn. On one hand, Kahanamoku was glad to be traveling. He'd just walked off another servile job in Honolulu, was nearly broke, and knew there would be no worthwhile employment prospects when he returned home the following month. On the other hand, he missed his family and friends, as well as his surf club. He also knew that the Moana Hotel at Waikiki was presently filled with record numbers of wealthy, good-looking tourists visiting from the Mainland—which, for a freelance surfing and swimming instructor, meant opportunities for business and light romance. Waikiki would always be Kahanamoku's seat of comfort. Now 5,000 miles from home, he often let his mind drift back to the few acres of water, reef, sand, and shade between Diamond Head and the south-shore beachfront—a celestial field for Kahanamoku and perhaps 200 other early-modern surfers.

But Freshwater was nonetheless having a therapeutic effect on Kahanamoku's homesickness and work problems. The Australian weather was agreeable. Swimming officials who had sponsored his trip saw that he was comfortably housed and well fed. The Sydney newspapers praised the "Bronzed Islander" as a paragon of sportsmanship and character, and the often belligerent Australian race fans had with some grace accepted him as inarguably superior to the local talent.

And, finally, Kahanamoku was about to give the host country its first demonstration of stand-up surfing. He had already become surfing's first and foremost nation-builder, founding a settlement of wave-riders in Atlantic City two years earlier. He would do the same in Australia and New Zealand and would later lift California surfing from relative obscurity to statewide—and, before long, nationwide—attention. He was a generous performer; a wave-sliding demonstration was usually followed by a casual beachside seminar on technique and board construction. Just as important, surfing as presented by Kahanamoku looked dignified and elegant, as well as great fun. His Olympic stature and his elevated presence transferred directly to the new sport and helped inoculate it against the vagaries of whim and fashion. Hollywood "beach movies" of the early 1960s would show surfing as young and frivolous—a depiction that wasn't entirely wrong. But during the first half of the century, a growing international fraternity of surfers followed Kahanamoku's lead and practiced a more courtly version of the sport.

Duke Kahanamoku didn't single-handedly bring surfing back from the dead, as some accounts have it, but his life so neatly parallels the sport's

Duke surfing Waikiki on a solid redwood "plank," probably 8 or 9 feet long and weighing about 75 pounds. In 1930 Kahanamoku built himself a sleek, 16-foot board that weighed 126 pounds. He rode it for twenty years. Tom Blake, the second most influential surfer of the early 20th century, remembers that Kahanamoku's water skills improved with age: "I would say that Duke attained his greatest surfing satisfactions and some of his greatest achievements as a rider after his 40th year."

Four of the six Kahanamoku brothers, plus some of their Waikiki beachboy friends, in front of the Moana Hotel, in 1928. Duke, the oldest brother, had posed a few minutes earlier alongside his siblings, then opted out of this less formal shot.

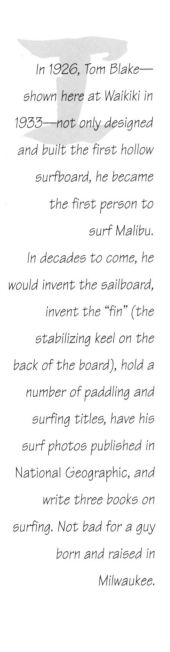

In 1926, Tom Blake—
shown here at Waikiki in
1933—not only designed
and built the first hollow
surfboard, he became
the first person to
surf Malibu.
In decades to come, he
would invent the sailboard,
invent the "fin" (the
stabilizing keel on the
back of the board), hold a
number of paddling and
surfing titles, have his
surf photos published in
National Geographic, and
write three books on
surfing. Not bad for a guy
born and raised in
Milwaukee.

revival that finer distinctions seem unnecessary. Just 30 years before Kahanamoku's visit to Australia, as Hawaiians impassively marked off their first hundred years of Anglo-Saxon contact, surfboards had nearly vanished from the beaches of Waikiki. So had much of the native population, for that matter. The Hawaiians' collective immune system had been virtually useless before the host of parasites that jumped ashore with the newcomers. Measles, small pox, syphilis, and other diseases freely moved from village to village and cut the indigenous population from 400,000 upon Captain Cook's arrival in 1778 to 40,000 at the time of Kahanamoku's birth in 1890. Parallel damage was done to economic, religious, and social practices—surfing included. "The sport," Jack London wrote in 1916, looking back, "was at its dying gasp. Not only did the Hawaiian-born not talk about it, but they forgot about it."

Open-sea fishermen, through the centuries, on coastlines around the world, no doubt rode waves to shore as they brought in the day's catch. But before the 20th century, only the Pacific Islanders built and rode special boards for surfing. By the time Cook arrived, Hawaiian surfers had advanced well beyond everyone else in the Polynesian group—hardly surprising, given that each island in the Hawaiian chain is surrounded by consistent, high-quality surf, and that the sport was practiced by men and women, royalty and commoners, children and grandparents.

This was genuine surf culture. Temples were dedicated to surfing, villages stood empty when a swell was running, and surfing festivals were staged annually. Fortunes were made and lost in competitions; an Oahu champion beat his Kauai rival and sailed home with a prize of 4,000 wild pigs and 16 war canoes. The stakes could go much higher. A day of high sport might end with the losing surfer's entrails laid out across the winning surfer's private altar. Surfing fables were told and retold, of kings, queens, princes, maidens, talking sharks, giant waves, new loves, infidelities, magic spells, and curses. In the water, a man and woman surfing side by side began their own romantic adventure—with the understanding that by sharing the same wave they'd moved to the final level of foreplay and would now head directly to shore for a round of lovemaking.

In 1778, Cook's lieutenant, James King, looked with an empirical eye on what he called the "great art" of surfing and noted that local wave riders "seem to feel a great pleasure in the motion which this exercise gives." Early British explorers and missionaries generally sent home favorable accounts of surfing. But when crusading New England missionaries arrived in 1820, the "great art" was recast as "heathen sport" and viewed as little more than an invitation to sex, gambling, and injury. Had the Americans arrived 40 years earlier and met a robust native population, they might have been turned back to the States—if not clubbed to death, as Cook had been after overstaying his welcome on the Big Island.

July 1941: a crowded summer day at San Onofre, at the far north end of San Diego County. These long, soft-breaking waves were the nearest thing California surfers had to Waikiki, and the Pacific Coast Surfriding Championships were held at San Onofre not long after this shot was taken. The hugely talented Pete Peterson won the contest. Following America's entry into World War II, the Championships were canceled from 1942 to 1946.

But the Hawaiian ranks had already been thinned by disease, native deities seemed fallible before the Christian God, and once-powerful local chiefs were unable to organize any real resistance. The missionaries in 10 short years convinced the Hawaiians to take up Calvinist-based religion, politics, and culture. Surfing wasn't categorically prohibited, but it was boxed out by the new work ethic, along with restrictions on nudity, gaming, and nearly all mixed-sex recreation. Just a few surfers were practicing regularly by the middle of the century. By 1892, an observer noted, it was "hard to find a surfboard outside of our museums and private collections."

But policy on surfing was beginning to change when Duke Paoa Kahanamoku—the first of nine children, the son of a Honolulu policeman, and the grandson of a retainer to King Kamehameha III—began surfing in Waikiki just before the turn of the century with a few of his school-age friends. His timing was excellent. American businessmen, having replaced the missionaries as Hawaii's wardens, correctly recognized that the sport might stoke the burgeoning tourist trade. Mark Twain had already visited the islands and was hugely impressed when a local surfer came "whizzing by like a bombshell!" Jack London, visiting Waikiki in 1907, portrayed himself honestly in his forthcoming article for *A Women's Home Companion* as a sunburned kook after his first day of surfing, but he graciously described the act as "a royal sport for the natural kings of earth."

Southern California beaches were meanwhile experiencing a recreational and commercial growth similar to that in Honolulu and Waikiki. A few months before London's article was published, Kahanamoku's close friend George Freeth, a 23-year-old Irish-Hawaiian surfer, was hired by developer Henry Huntington and brought to Redondo Beach. There he was billed as "the man who can walk on water" and sent into the surf to promote the new Los Angeles–Redondo railroad line. Freeth, however, wasn't the first Mainland surfer. Three visiting Hawaiians had previously had what amounted to a prehistoric surf session in the 1880s, taking their redwood planks into the wintry 50-degree waves near the San Lorenzo rivermouth in Santa Cruz. But the locals showed no interest in taking up the sport themselves, and the event was forgotten for more than a hundred years. Freeth had better luck, thanks to the mellow Southern California climate and the considerable advertising strength of Huntington. Hundreds of Los Angeles residents took the Red Car southwest to its Redondo terminus, disembarked, and stood in the sand to watch Freeth give surfing demonstrations. Small colonies of surfers popped up immediately in the nearby beach towns.

Three years later, in 1910, Kahanamoku raised the sport's performance level after making himself a streamlined 10-foot surfboard—about 2 feet bigger than the day's standard. The new board not only rode faster and smoother, it paddled like a dream, and when the surf was up, Kahanamoku was able to investigate the distant fringe of the Waikiki reefs where the waves were bigger, steeper, and more critical.

Hoppy Swarts (opposite page) was photographed by John Heath "Doc" Ball in the late 1930s. Ball's indispensable photographs of the fledgling West Coast surf scene were collected in a book titled California Surfriders, originally published in 1946. "The purpose of this volume," Ball wrote in his foreword, "is to present pictorially some of the thrills, spills, and places pertinent to surfriding, which is now becoming California's favorite saltwater sport." (Below) Santa Cruz surfers would retire to the clubhouse to warm up after a dip in the chilly Northern California water.

(The limit of modern surfing's bigger-is-better principal of surf-board design was reached in 1930, when Kahanamoku built a semi-hollow, missile-shaped redwood board that measured 16 feet and weighed 126 pounds.)

Meanwhile, the sport's popularity was also growing. In 1911, membership in the 4-year-old Outrigger Canoe and Surfing Club numbered in the hundreds. Kahanamoku himself was captain and cofounder of the just-established Hui Nalu surf club. That year he wrote a front-page article on surfing in the premier issue of *Mid-Pacific Magazine*. "I have never seen snow," Kahanamoku began, "and do not know what winter means . . . but every day of the year, where the water is 76, day and night, and the waves roll high, I take my sled, without runners, and coast down the face of the big waves that roll in at Waikiki."

Kahanamoku, then 21, a part-time stevedore, was first among equals with the Waikiki set—no small honor for a surfer. National celebrity came to him that summer after Hawaii's first Amateur Athletic Union–sanctioned swim meet when Kahanamoku, untrained and competing for the first time, broke the 100-yard freestyle world record by more than four seconds, putting a 30-foot gap between himself and the runner-up. Less than an hour later he broke the 50-yard record by more than a second and a half.

In 1912 he won a gold medal in the 1912 Olympics in Stockholm, and before the Games were finished, Kahanamoku, through style and presence as much as athleticism, had become a European sensation. It helped that "Duke" often registered in the Old World as a title rather than a given name, allowing him an up-front measure of deference and respect. And even if Kahanamoku was a nearly inarticulate ninth-grade dropout, he did in fact have a noble bearing. He could look dignified even as he hunched his 6-foot, 2-inch, 183-pound frame around a tiny wooden ukulele between races at Stockholm, his giant hands strumming casually. Outside the arena, he dressed like an Oxford graduate in a tailored suit, high-collared dress shirt, and silk tie. The case may have been overstated when Kahanamoku was described by an American sculptor as "the most magnificent human male that God ever put on the earth," but he was attractive by any standard—powerful, gentle, and exotic, with high, slanting cheekbones, dark eyes, and a wide, full-lipped mouth. He had a calming presence. His biggest smile, rarely practiced, sent out near-visible waves of kindness and warmth.

Kahanamoku spent several months after the Olympics traveling

Makaha, located on the west side of Oahu, was one of the first discoveries made by Honolulu surfers when they ventured out of Waikiki, exploring the perimeter of the island for good surf. By 1957, when these two shots were taken (below and right), Makaha was known as the most versatile break in the world, with good waves rolling in from 2 to 20 feet. Visiting surfers often stayed the winter in Army Quonset huts left over from the war.

through Europe and mainland America, then finally returned to Honolulu, stepping off the boat as the Royal Hawaiian Band played on the dock and cannons were fired in salute. Elsewhere, the reception hadn't been nearly so welcoming. Skin color had been an issue during Kahanamoku's travels, especially through continental America. He was refused service by restaurant owners. His Polynesian features often stumped the provincials, as they tried to figure out whether to slander him as a black man or an Indian. The sporting press, meanwhile, still overlooked him in favor of George Cunha, Kahanamoku's friend and teammate—who was referred to in print as "the world's finest white sprint swimmer."

New problems came up when Kahanamoku returned to Hawaii. He could only find menial work in Honolulu, and in late 1912, just weeks after being feted in one European capital city after another, he was working as a meter reader on Honolulu city streets. Perhaps Hawaii didn't owe him a job. But nonetheless there seemed to be a moral and financial imbalance when local officials, the Chamber of Commerce, and the Hawaii Promotion Committee all acknowledged Kahanamoku's part in making Hawaii one of the world's premier tourist destinations, then refused to cut him in on the proceeds. Yet Kahanamoku never lost his sense of obligation to his home state. For decades he served as a Honolulu city greeter and escort. Babe Ruth, Shirley Temple, Mickey Rooney, Groucho Marx, Prince Edward, Arthur Godfrey, and President Kennedy—all were met and squired by Kahanamoku when visiting Hawaii, and all were touched by his gracious, playful, definitive aloha style. When the British Queen Mother arrived in Honolulu in 1966, she accepted a flower lei from the white-haired surfer as Hawaiian music played in the background, and moments later the two began an impromptu hula.

Kahanamoku struggled constantly with his schizophrenic career. When he wasn't defending his title as the world's fastest swimmer (after Stockholm, he won medals in the 1920 and 1924 Games) or being cast in bit parts in Hollywood movies (appearing as an Indian chief in one film and a Turkish sultan in another but generally playing the loyal and exotic manservant), Kahanamoku swept the floors and mowed the lawn at City Hall. He also worked the chains for a surveying team, pumped gas, then held office for nearly three decades as the sheriff of the City and County of Honolulu—another low-paying job, despite the big title. In his last few years, Kahanamoku was able to trade in successfully on his name, but in a 1961 *Honolulu Star-Bulletin* article, the 71-year-old, with a quiet bitterness, summarized his past and present financial condition: "I am barely getting along."

While money problems were an enduring feature of Kahanamoku's adult life, there were, of course, opportunities that came with being the world

Kahanamoku won the 100-meter freestyle swimming gold medal in the 1912 Olympic Games in Stockholm. Eight years later (World War I forced the cancellation of the 1916 Games), Kahanamoku, age 30, sailed to Antwerp for the 1920 Olympics, where he won another 100-meter freestyle gold medal. He also played on the U.S. water polo team, in water so cold that "I couldn't feel anything," he later said. "I could hardly do my little trick of holding some of these guys down with both my feet."

1920 Olympics   Antwerp

Kahanamoku served as the unofficial "Honolulu greeter" for decades, and when Shirely Temple visited Hawaii in 1935, he lifted the 7-year-old child star up on his shoulders. Years earlier, Kahanamoku gave the same treatment to a young surfer at Waikiki.

swimming champion. Such was the case in late 1914, when the New South Wales Swimming Association invited the young Kahanamoku to Australia for a 33-race swimming tour. Kahanamoku gratefully accepted. Australian officials were just as appreciative; the Hawaiian swimmer would be the first visiting Olympic gold medalist, and it was hoped that he would provide a small diversion from Australia's recent entry into the First World War.

Kahanamoku arrived in Sydney on December 14 after a 2-week boat trip, and a few days later agreed, when asked by local swimming organizers, to give a surfing demonstration. Date and site were quickly determined—Wednesday, December 23, Freshwater Beach, just north of Sydney. Expectations were peaking in the days before the exhibition, fed by word-of-mouth and newspaper stories. "Kahanamoku," reported *The Sydney Referee*, "is a wonderfully dexterous performer on the surfboard, an instrument of pleasure that Australians have so far been unsuccessful in handling to any degree. Reports have been brought back from overseas of his acrobatic feats executed while dashing shorewards at great speeds."

The Wednesday morning surf check found some passable waves at Freshwater. By 10:00 A.M. the summer sun had warmed the beach, and two or three hundred spectators were lined up along the shoreline, with dozens more settled in on the nearby headland. Kahanamoku arrived at 10:30. He moved across the sand toward the ocean in a standard black, one-piece swimsuit, with his new board resting easily on his right shoulder. Members of the local surf-rescue club, in a sincere but countrified offer, said they'd tow his board through the waves in their surfboat. Kahanamoku said he could manage. The lifesavers nonetheless trailed Kahanamoku as he walked across the wet sand into the surf. Seconds later, paddling through the lines of broken waves, he distanced himself from the local convoy and soon pulled up alone in the calm water outside the surf line. He sat on his board and watched the ocean for a few moments. A swell moved in. He rotated to face shoreward, went prone, paddled, waited as his forward movement was amplified by the wave's energy, then pushed to his feet. New board, new spot, first time surfing in a month—Kahanamoku set an easy course to his left and simply let the wave push him into shallow water.

Years later 16-year-old Claude West of Manly Beach would speak of Kahanamoku's first ride in phrases usually associated with religious conversion. But at the moment he simply watched, felt the excitement flood up, then burst into cheers along with the rest of the crowd. The noise moved across the surf. "I must have

DUKE P. KAHANAMOKU

UNION GASOLINE

At age 42, Kahanamoku played for the U.S. water polo team in the 1932 Olympics in Los Angeles. Then, after returning to Hawaii, he spent two years managing a pair of Union gas stations. The work was often demeaning. Some customers would ask Kahanamoku to clean their windshield, then photograph the world-famous athlete as he leaned into his menial work. Friends, meanwhile, gently poked fun at him with a little song they made up: "Duke Kahanamoku, Former Olympic Champion, Now Pumping Gas."

Kahanamoku comes to the end of one of his Freshwater rides. The ocean brought out an impetuous side of this quiet, gracious man. In 1912, when the steamer New York had some engine trouble and stalled in the middle of the Atlantic, Kahanamoku put on his bathing suit and jumped over the railing for a swim. The ship quickly drifted away on the current, and a lifeboat had to be sent out to rescue the Olympic hero.

put on a show that more than trapped their fancy," Kahanamoku later wrote, "for the crowds on shore applauded me loud and long." Energized by the response, and glad to once again be on the surf beat, Kahanamoku stayed in the water for more than an hour, now comfortable on his new board as he angled left, then right, before sending his audience into mild group hysteria when he brought the first part of his performance to a close with a headstand.

Surrounded by onlookers back on the beach, Kahanamoku asked for a tandem partner. Minutes later, he was again stationed past the surf line with Freshwater's Isabel Letham, a 15-year-old already known as a fine swimmer and bodysurfer. A wave moved in. Kahanamoku paddled while Letham hung on to the sides of the board. "When we got onto the crest of this wave," she later recalled, "and I looked down into the trough, I thought I was going over a cliff." Letham shouted for Kahanamoku to stop, and he back-paddled to stall the board. Another wave, and again Letham balked. A few minutes later—same thing. Finally Kahanamoku ignored her, pressed forward, stood, and hauled Letham to her feet. "After that," she remembered, "I was all right."

A stiff and overarticulated bronze statue of Duke Kahanamoku was dedicated in Freshwater in 1994. The gesture was heartfelt, but not likely to put any warmth, blood, and humanity back into a name that for most surfers had long ago been flattened by history. Although Kahanamoku is still revered as the embodiment of the warm and generous (and now largely symbolic) "aloha spirit," it may be convenience, as much as honor, that supports his title as the Father of Modern Surfing. But for those who recognize him as a composite athlete, traveler, adventurer, and sex idol, gratifying connections can be made between Kahanamoku and his surfing progeny. Phil Edwards, Nat Young, and Tom Carroll, like Kahanamoku, knew that good technique was reducible to a balance between raw power and elegance. David Nuuhiwa, Wayne Bartholomew, and Kelly Slater, like Kahanamoku, left their cash-poor existence behind when they went surfing. Bob Simmons and Tom Curren—and the nation of surfers in general—are, like Kahanamoku, slightly mysterious outsiders. And today, as baby-boomer surfers angle through the rough waters of middle-age, they might find solace in the fact that Kahanamoku surfed into his 70s and even spoke metaphorically near the end of his life about soon being able to "pick the right kind of wave and keep on riding."

Kahanamoku's Australian swimming tour continued into January of 1915. Before sailing for New Zealand, and then home, he visited Sydney's Dee Why Beach for a final day in the surf. Isabel Letham was ready for her second tandem demonstration—this time executing start to finish without hesitation. Teenager Claude West, meanwhile, was again on the beach watching, and by some combination of tactical maneuvering and luck was at Kahanamoku's elbow as the Hawaiian prepared to leave. Kahanamoku handed the sugar-pine board to West, who would soon become the first in a dynasty of Australian surfing champions. 🏄

Kahanamoku is shown here minutes before his 1914 Freshwater exhibition. He was so popular in Australia that the Sydney papers would occasionally place the most recent Kahanamoku news above the latest report from the Great War in Europe.

SURFARI

In Search of the Perfect Wave

Bruce Brown, Robert August, and Mike Hynson found perfect surf at Cape St. Francis, South Africa, in late November 1963, and the discovery, as presented in Brown's film *The Endless Summer,* is as much a part of surfing history and lore as a story from the Old Testament. The surfers involved were real. The setting was real. But the discovery, as it appears onscreen, was a masterfully created illusion. Perfect surf is rare, even wondrous, and the movie's brief Cape St. Francis episode shimmers as it comes and goes, like a dream.

"It was about three miles across these sand dunes to the water," recounts Bruce Brown's Southern California voice, familiar to millions, on the *Endless Summer* soundtrack as the Cape St. Francis sequence begins. "We had no idea what was on the other side," he continues, "but we'd come halfway around the world, so we thought we'd take a look." And off they go, barefoot and wearing just surf trunks, carrying their boards. The dunes, in this vast, uninhabited corner of Africa, are smooth and endless. The desert sun presses down, directly overhead. Brown tells us that the odds of locating good surf were ridiculously long. They weren't even sure they'd find water. Then more dunes. More hot sun. Fatigue. The group then breaks into a jog before reaching the top of the last dune overlooking the ocean. Brown shows us the surfers' stunned reaction, then cuts to an overview shot. A cloudless sky fills the top half of the screen, the bottom edge is defined by a rocky beach, and a single wave is stretched across the middle like a blue-green ribbon. A desert wind blows against the crest and throws a light filigree of spray into the air. The curl pours over so evenly that the wave seems to be standing still. Hynson and August, recovered from their initial shock, rush forward across the beach. Hynson

gets the first ride and, to his eternal credit, spends much of his time standing in perfect trim, nearly motionless, feet together, back straight, humming along with the wave like a tuning fork. "On Mike's first ride, the first 5 seconds," Brown narrates, playing out an exquisite moment, "he knew he'd finally found that perfect wave."

The Endless Summer has always been viewed as the crowning event in the time-honored search for perfect surf. Twenty-five years after he rode Cape St. Francis, Mike Hynson, now weathered and somewhat irascible, wondered aloud if the search wasn't in fact created by Brown's movie. "If

The Endless Summer poster began with this black-and-white photograph (left) of Bruce Brown, Mike Hynson, and Robert August, shot at Capistrano Beach in Southern California. Graphic designer John Van Hammersveld then "posterized" the shot, added a setting sun, and divided the background colors into neon orange, pink, and yellow. The resulting Endless Summer promo piece would become surfing's most famous image. (Opposite page) Brown and crew, en route to Cape St. Francis. (Previous spread) A moment of high adventure in Baja California.

we didn't make *The Endless Summer*, do you think there would even be this quest for the perfect wave? Huh? You think anybody would even care?" It's a good question. At the very least, *The Endless Summer* had a great amplifying effect. Surfers had long been diligent in looking for new places to ride, but not until Brown's movie did the search take on a Holy Grail fervor.

Wild adventures followed. Surf travel, magnifying a principle of travel in general, lent itself to extremes, and surfers regularly brought home incredible stories of fortune, romance, danger, and idiocy. Photographer Alby Falzon glanced to his left during an afternoon sight-seeing visit to a Balinese temple in 1971 and discovered the gorgeous surf of Uluwatu. A tidal wave exploded over a group of surfers camped on the edge of a Javanese wildlife preserve and rolled them 75 yards into the jungle. Brazilian surfer Adrian Kojin left Huntington Beach at midnight, on a motorcycle, carrying a bedroll and a surfboard, and spent eight months camping and surfing along the southern perimeter of Central and South America. A visiting surfer woke up in the midafternoon after a lunatic night of drinking in a Third World country, discovered a coarse row of sutures on his lower back, and found out that one of his kidneys had been stolen.

Yet despite these celebrated adventures, it may be that the greatest product of surf exploration is tedium. Tom Curren, after spending three years in the early 1990s flying, driving, and sailing from country to country searching for waves, couldn't bear the idea of a fourth year of travel. "Just to think of it," he said, "bores me to tears."

But in general, the post–*Endless Summer* rush to distant shores has continued without letup. In the early 1980s, corporate-sponsored professionals surfed exotic waves alongside nomadic counterculture holdouts, some of whom had been on the road for years. Not long after, recreational surfers with a good line of credit could, with a phone call, book themselves for a long weekend into exotic and expensive surf resorts.

The character of the perfect wave itself has changed with time. The long and gentle surf of Waikiki, Hawaii, was the ideal medium for the heavy-ballast redwood boards used in the first half of the century, and back then, a surfer's vision of earthly paradise was a side-on view of Diamond Head surrounded by ocean and surf. Decades later, the lighter longboards of the 1950s and 1960s (first made of balsa wood, then polyurethane foam, all with a stabilizing fin) inspired dreams of the finely tapered waves of Malibu, in Southern California. Surfing maneuvers changed with board design, and rudimentary "sliding" gave way to whip-turns, kick-stalls, and hanging ten. Perfection became a hot summer swell at Malibu, when a surfer could run through his entire repertoire two or three times on a single wave.

When board size dropped from 10 feet to 7 feet during the

Tom Curren won the world title in 1985, 1986, and 1990, then retired from full-time competition. He traveled often in the years to follow and in 1994 came upon this break (opposite), known as Fish Bowls, somewhere in the Indian Ocean. "Dawn revealed a dreamscape," Curren wrote a few weeks later. "I swear I didn't even want to look at it before paddling out for fear of being paralyzed by the sheer beauty." (Below) Discovering surf in Morocco, 1975.

Until the late 1960s, the precise location of each newly discovered break was featured in the surf magazines. By the mid-1970s this was no longer true, since overcrowding had begun to touch even the more remote areas of the surf world. When this Indonesian spot (below) was first shown in Surfer Magazine, its location was given as "one of the outer islands, a long boat ride from Bali."
(Opposite page) Taylor Knox, Costa Rica.
(Following spread) Australian Shane Powell surfs another unidentified spot in Indonesia.

shortboard revolution of the late 1960s, the dream was transformed again. This time, the tube-ride—angling through the chambered area between the face of the wave and the descending curl—became the supreme moment in surfing. Tube-ride descriptions quickly spun out of control, as the experience was metaphorically linked to sex, birth, touchdowns, and God. But, in fairness, the sensation of riding untouched through a revolving column of water went far beyond anything surfers had previously experienced, and by 1970, the mandate was clear: spend as much time as possible in the tube (or "the Pope's living room," as a top surfer of the period described it). The new version of the perfect wave had to be cylindrical, hollow, and tubular. Malibu was no longer challenging enough. On the other hand, the beautiful but deadly waves of the Banzai Pipeline in Hawaii were viewed by most surfers as tubular to a fault. Burleigh Heads and Kirra, both located on Queensland's Gold Coast, seemed to split the difference between Malibu and Pipeline, and by the mid-1970s the two breaks were hoisted as the new perfect wave standard, along with South Africa's Jeffreys Bay. Grajagan, located on the southern tip of Java, was added to the short list a few years later.

Discovery, of course, has invited ruin. In the late 1950s, when the "perfect wave" designation floated above Malibu like a neon sign, surfers were banging off one another in the lineup like heated molecules. To varying degrees, the same would eventually hold true for Pipeline, Kirra, Jeffreys, Grajagan, and any other spot renowned and cursed as "perfect." For many surfers, in fact, the real search for the perfect wave has always had less to do with adventure, romance, and the pursuit of new experiences and more with just getting the hell away from what long-suffering Malibu legend Mickey Dora called "all the surf dopes, ego heroes, rah-rah boys, concessionaires, lifeguards, fags, and finks." Surfers on the road didn't look for anything particularly different. They wanted Malibu (or Kirra, or Grajagan, etc.) without the crowds.

So advanced troops, in small numbers, have marched steadily into the unknown to try to re-create more or less what has been lost at home. Discoveries—some fantastic, others just novel—have been made in recent years in Indonesia, the Philippines, the Maldives, Alaska, Iceland, New Guinea, and China. Meanwhile, the huge majority of surfers settle into domesticity with their local beach and look forward perhaps to an annual two-week vacation at one or another well-established surf colony. In the intervening months, they may travel briefly and vicariously through surf films and magazines. John Severson, who founded *Surfer* in 1960, capitalized on this longing for distant and unpopulated perfection. In many ways, the magazine was a print version of *The Endless Summer*: "It's a dream magazine," Severson said years later. "I saw that right away. The perfect surf, the faraway places . . . we all dream about the same things."

Taylor Knox surfs Cloud Nine in the Philippines. Surf-seeking often meant first-rate waves and Third World accommodations: "A lady from the village had some beachfront huts for rent," Knox recalled. "No running water and a bare bulb hanging from the ceiling. The bathroom was an open hole we flushed with a bucket of water." The waves, though, were great for 2 weeks straight. "It never got under 6 feet . . . a guaranteed barrel every time."

Which brings us back to Bruce Brown, Mike Hynson, Robert August, Cape St. Francis, and the real alchemy of surf travel: reality heightened by imagination.

Brown understood this better than anyone. He was just 26 when he filmed *The Endless Summer*, but he'd already made four full-length surf films. He knew that *The Endless Summer* was a make-or-break movie, since the $50,000 he'd staked on the project represented the earnings from all his previous films plus all that he could borrow. He also fully realized the utility and potential of the production process. So while the surf footage at Cape St. Francis did fall into Brown's hands like a dirt-encrusted jewel, it wasn't until months later, when it was scrupulously cut, edited, and scored, that it revealed itself as the ultimate surf fantasy. Brevity was a key. The entire Cape St. Francis episode, sand dunes included, is just 6 minutes long and shows only fifteen waves. But each image is expertly framed, composed, and attached with care to its neighboring shots, and the entire sequence is scored by a lovely, original instrumental melody. Finally, of course, there is Brown's seductive narration: the water, he tells us, is 70 degrees, the prevailing winds blow offshore, and the waves are this good 300 days a year. Hynson and August, he asserts, were able to lock themselves in the curl for 45 seconds at a time, and rides were so long that most wouldn't fit on one piece of film. Brown continues: on a big day, a surfer might catch a 15-foot wave at the top of the Cape and make it all the way to the bottom—a mind-boggling 7-mile ride.

By this point in the film, Brown has become such a friend to his audience that everything he says registers as accurate and confirmed, even though he has long since crossed the line over to art, or deception, or both.

Quality surf and spare accommodations describe the Grajagan surf camp, on the edge of a jungle preserve near the eastern tip of Java. The entire area is referred to as "G-Land," and the break itself has, over the past 15 years, become emblematic of the perfect wave: 300-yard-long rides are common, and the practiced surfer can disappear into the tube almost at will.

Setting the factual record straight, the prevailing wind at Cape St. Francis is not offshore, and a surfer would be more likely to see a troupe of hula dancers gyrate across the Cape than a set of clean 15-foot waves peeling off for 7 miles. Brown's 300-good-surf-days-a-year claim was overstated by about 285 days. He relied on an even higher degree of poetic license to create the dune-filled "discovery" sequence. Two days earlier, after a long drive through the South African interior, Brown and his team had arrived at the base of the Cape and checked into a small vacation resort. The next morning, while Hynson and August rode a few mediocre waves in front of their rooms, an outgoing tide produced what appeared to be a shapely wave about 1 mile to the southwest. A quick walk up the beach led them to Cape St. Francis, where they filmed for just 90 minutes until the wind and tide changed and the surf quit. The next day Brown staged the famous march-for-the-cameras across the dunes. The day after that they were back on the road.

It might be said that the entire *Endless Summer* project was born in deception,

starting with the title. Brown knew that the best waves are found in winter, not summer. But he also knew that Midwesterners would never drive through sleet and snow to see a movie called *The Endless Winter*.

One year after Brown found Cape St. Francis, *The Endless Summer* began its remarkable cinematic rise. A 16mm version of the film toured the surf-city circuit in 1964. The following year it was screen-tested in Wichita, Kansas, and was a smash hit. In 1966 it was blown up to 35mm and put into general release, where it earned about $7 million.

New York reviewers, like doting aunts, rushed in and smothered Brown's little movie with affection—although some did so with less condescension than others. *Newsweek* acknowledged Brown's melding of fact and fiction and labeled the movie a "celebration of surf," which was exactly right. Had it been an authentic "documentary" (as *The New Yorker* and *Time* generously described it), *The Endless Summer* would have been a different film entirely. None of the journey's hardships turned up onscreen. In reality, money was tight, the surf, with a few exceptions, was lousy, and boredom and irritability were recycled constantly. The cocky expression Hynson wore as he popped up in Ghana, Australia, New Zealand, and Tahiti was due in part to the Benzedrine he'd stashed in his suitcase (alongside a baggie of pot), his ongoing international sex sampling, and the fact that he'd put a comfortable distance between himself and his U.S. Army induction papers. Furthermore, Brown, Hynson, and August experienced a uniquely powerful moment of homesickness, just days before they discovered Cape St. Francis, when President Kennedy was shot.

A movie taking into account all of these moods and events would have been a lot closer to surf travel as it's really been experienced over the decades. But the spirit of the film would have been snuffed out in the process.

Robert August always knew that it was timing, outlook, and emotion, not accuracy, that put *The Endless Summer* over the top in 1966. Brown's film followed on the heels of Gidget and the Beach Boys, but *The Endless Summer*, August says, may have connected with its audience on a different level than any previous surf-culture experience. "It was the Vietnam era," he remembers. "Everything was controversial; everything was tense. And Bruce's movie was like a big time-out. It was like: 'let's just go to the beach and have fun.'"

With *The Endless Summer*, Cape St. Francis became surfing's greatest shared dream. Bigger, longer, faster, hollower waves were found in years to come, but none fit as neatly into surfing's collective consciousness. For that, credit goes not only to Brown for his artful presentation, but to the unseen meteorological hand that allowed just 90 minutes of quality

Tavarua Island in Fiji (opposite page) has become famous as a high-end adventure package for surfers. For $135 a day (airfare not included), a limited number of visitors, for a predetermined length of time, are housed, fed, entertained, and deposited by boat at scheduled times at the surf break. (Below) Once in the water, of course, surfers have a completely unscripted Tavarua experience.

Evan Slater and Taylor Knox kick back one afternoon in the tropics (right). Are they relaxed and sated or bored senseless? Are they feeling an atavistic connection to primordial forebears or an overpowering desire for a Whopper with cheese? Floridian surfer CJ Hobgood surfs in the Maldive Islands (opposite page), a chain of small coral atolls in the Indian Ocean, about 400 miles below the southern tip of India.

Although Jeffreys Bay in South Africa has long been one of surfing's ultimate destinations, there's no guarantee that visiting surfers will find great waves, as demonstrated by these entries from a Jeffreys hotel guest book: Shaun Tomson, 1968: "Outasight. Stoked." Ian Wallis, 1968: "6 days no surf." Dick Hoole, 1977: "10 feet and perfect when we arrived, and perfect a week later when we left." Stinkfoot, 1979: "I'm not impressed at all. Yankee go home."

surf during his visit to Cape St. Francis. Fifteen waves doesn't add up to much screen time. But surfers don't really expect any more. Their natural state is one of longing and partially filled desire, and for the most part, they hope for nothing more than a few exceptional days a year. Furthermore, a great afternoon of surfing might break down to less than 2 minutes of actual time spent up and riding. Their imagination, in other words, has to take up a lot of slack. But an outlook that relies heavily on fantasy can wear exceptionally well.

Perfection, in fact, almost has to be ephemeral. Thirty years after *The Endless Summer* debuted, an expedition to the Philippines discovered a flawless right-breaking tube, which was quickly given the suitably romantic name of Cloud Nine. Conditions were both extraordinary and unchanging for 14 consecutive days, and the visitors extended themselves to the utmost. "It was satisfying for a while—an incredible wave," one of the surfers wrote. "But even perfection gets monotonous after a couple of weeks."

Few people in the history of surfing, of course, have found themselves in this position. For the most part, lifetime surfers carry on happily in part because there is always an exceptional, one-of-a-kind day of surfing somewhere in the future. Meanwhile, the daily rhythm of surfing, even with the crowds, clears the mind, provides exercise, and the occasional moment of grace.

Perfection in surfing, for most, is a lovely fiction that now and again becomes truth. This is why the brief and largely invented Cape St. Francis discovery has such an authentic feel. And this is why Mike Hynson is right to demur when asked for a detailed account of his visit to Cape St. Francis. "Naw, I'd rather keep the mystique going," he responds. "You figure it out for yourself. You see a wave like that after you haven't surfed for 2 weeks. . . ." He wants to say more, then catches himself and smiles. "It was a dream come true, man. It was heaven."

Robert August and Cape St. Francis both starred in the movie The Endless Summer. *Although the surf only lasted 90 minutes, filmmaker Bruce Brown made the most of it, and Cape St. Francis would soon become a shared fantasy for surfers everywhere.*

California surfers of the late 1950s and early 1960s drove south into Mexico and were disappointed time and again by the size and consistency of the waves. Interest in Mexico was revived with the 1965 discovery of the "Mexican Malibu," and by the time the "Mexican Pipeline"—later known as Puerto Escondido—was uncovered in the late 1970s, the country's surfing reputation had turned around completely. Allen Johnson (opposite page) surfs Puerto Escondido in 1994. The Philippines' Cloud Nine (left) was first surfed in the early 1990s.

THE HEAT OF
COMPETITION

MASTERS OF THE UNIVERSE

Rob Machado glided serenely into a 6-by-6-foot tube during the semifinals of the Chiemsee Pipe Masters in Hawaii, the final event of the 1995 pro tour season. He disappeared for a moment, then his refracted image became visible on the exterior of the curl, like a shadow through frosted glass—clear enough that the 300 or so spectators watching from the shore could track his progress as he flowed through the hollows. Three seconds ticked off. A small buzz moved across the beach, as the opening at the end of the tube began to spiral in on itself. Four seconds. A sharp whistle of approval was heard from the audience, then another, as it seemed Machado himself was controlling the wave's shape, speed, and contour. Then, just as the wave expired in deep water, he popped back into the open. Moments later the score was announced—a perfect 10. Machado, at 20 minutes past noon, on December 18, 1995, had a loose grip on the world title crown. Meanwhile Kelly Slater, defending world champion, Machado's longtime friend and professional rival, was paddling into a wave that had bent itself into what looked like a huge, polished, concave piece of modern art. Slater pushed to his feet and leaned to his inside rail. The wave was bigger than Machado's, the drop more critical. Slater's route through the tube was deeper, faster, and longer, and the noise from the audience was raw, almost disbelieving, when he shot from the gorge back into sunlight. Another perfect 10 and another atmospheric jump in energy. At 21 minutes past noon, the score was tied, and the world title was again free-floating.

At that moment, professional surfing reached a level of fulfillment that it can never again touch. The Slater-Machado heat would be called the greatest ever seen—but that wasn't it, entirely. Other matchups

in years to come would be just as thrilling. The greater significance of the 1995 Pipeline Masters was symbolic. It was the culmination of a series of contests based on a new theory of competitive surfing—one that viewed good waves as an inviolable prerequisite, instead of a hoped-for luxury. The experiment worked beautifully. In seasons past, the entire pro surfing schedule might go by without a single worthwhile contest. By contrast, 1995 would feature six first-rate events. The world tour was pumped full of new purpose. Good surf first. It was that simple. The Pipeline Masters, founded 25 years earlier, had always known it. Now, finally, the rest of professional surfing had caught on.

Surfing competition reached a peak at the 1995 Chiemsee Pipe Masters in Hawaii, when Rob Machado and Kelly Slater tied with perfect 10s. "The contest didn't even matter at that point," Machado says. "It turned into two friends just having a great time. (Previous page) When this set came in, I said to Kelly, 'You want the first wave?' He said, 'Yeah, I'll take this one, you take the next one.' Paddling into it was a breeze, I don't think I could have messed that wave up if I tried. Then as I was riding, I could hear Kelly screaming and yelling. Can you see me smiling in the photos?" (Pages 52–54) Kelly Slater heads toward his third world title, during the 1995 Chiemsee Pipe Masters.

Gerry Lopez, surfing's own Godfather of Soul, helped bring the Pipeline Masters to life in the early 1970s. Nobody in the sport had greater status. When Lopez mailed off his first Masters entry form, it was nothing less than a benediction. In the years to follow, it often seemed as if the Masters was the only contest that understood and planned for a basic meteorological truth: good waves can't be scheduled. The field dictates the game, and surfing competition is worse than useless when surf conditions are poor. This is true for all surf locations, but especially at Pipeline, where a single afternoon of roaring deep-blue tubes will often be preceded by 2 or 3 weeks of rough, disorganized seas. The Pipeline Masters soon became the best contest in the world in part because it was held at a prized location, but also because it accepted the sport on its own imperious terms. Virtually all other pro contests were staged with fascist precision and planned out to the minute, waves or no waves. At Pipeline, surfers, journalists, and organizers had to show up and wait. The surf didn't always come. But the Masters delivered perhaps 3 years out of 4, and with some regularity the contest's best moments would stand as highlights for the entire surfing year.

Still, as recently as 1994, when Slater won his second world title in hopelessly wind-blown 3-foot surf, it looked as if the rest of competitive surfing would forever live in a state of uninspired ambivalence—not quite surfing and not quite a sporting event. Over the decades, most contests had failed to capture the interest of rank-and-file surfers, who tended to be satisfied with the unregulated nature of surfing. Surf magazines fed their cynicism with articles like "The Death of All Contests" and "Judge Not, That Ye Not Be Judged." Competitors themselves had made a kind of parlor game of trying to name the worst surf contest ever—usually a match between the 1972 world championships in San Diego and the 1985 wavepool contest at Allentown, Pennsylvania. Of the many and sundry bad decisions made in San Diego, the only one that really mattered was fumbling away a chance to move the contest a few miles north into excellent overhead surf at Trestles Beach. Instead, organizers chose to stay put and sent the finalists out into gurgling 2-foot windswell at Ocean Beach. Equally embarassing was the black comedy, 13 years later, of the World Professional Inland Surfing Championships, held at Allentown's Dorney Park and Wildwater Kingdom wavepool. Moments before the final heat, Derek Ho and Tom Carroll, the two best Pipeline surfers in the world, floated stoically in the deep end of the pool, their legs dangling in the chlorinated water, while they waited for submerged, diesel-driven flaps to send forth a half-hour program of feeble, miniature waves. Visitors to Wildwater Kingdom quickly passed judgment and were walking in a fairly steady stream away from the surf contest to the Kamikaze Plunge Speed Slide, 20 yards to the south.

Inevitably, a pro surfing career comes with these kinds of humiliating strings attached. Still, to one degree or another, it is a career. When the world pro circuit debuted in 1976 and was instantly made synonymous with competitive surfing, people were astounded to learn that the new professionals, perhaps a dozen of them, might soon be earning $20,000, even $30,000, a year in prize money and endorsement fees. Meanwhile,

Four-time world champion Kelly Slater has built a career out of fast, explosive, highly innovative surfing. As a preteen in Cocoa Beach, Florida, Slater already carried the burden of great expectations. His achievements throughout the 1990s, if anything, made all prophecies seem timid.

Martin Potter from South Africa (below) turned professional at age 16, but was too emotionally volatile to ever become world champion. For one season only, in 1989, Potter was able to stay focused on competition. He won the world title that year—easily. (Opposite page) California pro surfer Richie Collins reacts after being announced the winner of the 1988 O'Neill Cold Water Classic, in Santa Cruz, California.

sponsors and organizers, with dollar signs for eyes, gazed out at what they imagined was a dazzling new promotions and marketing frontier. Their original idea was to model pro surfing after pro football, with a scheduled Sunday afternoon climax and huge on-site crowds. Spectacle was valued over sport. By the late 1980s, $75,000 contests in Huntington Beach, Rio, Sydney, and Biarritz had surfers fighting for attention with beachside bungie jumpers, 50-foot inflatable soft drink bottles, bikini contests, autograph booths, and an endless loop of mega-amplified, low-common-denominator rock and roll. There were a few bright spots, however. The events occasionally took on a festive, Mardi Gras atmosphere. Local kids were always thrilled to see surfing's headliners at close range. And by the law of averages, a small number of world tour contests over the years (perhaps 1 in 10) actually met with good surf. But in general the surfing event promotors honored wave-riding the way shopping malls during Christmas rush honor religion.

Rob Machado, raised in the subdued coastal atmosphere of northern San Diego County, seemed to understand perfectly the distinction between the art of surfing and the artifice of competition when, at age 22, after 3 years as a well-paid professional, he said, "I'm doing everything I can to enjoy this whole career thing right now, but when I'm done I can go back to being a surfer." Mickey Dora's perspective was much the same in the summer of 1967 when, for his competitive surfing signoff, he dropped his trunks at the Malibu Invitational Surfing Contest and mooned the assembled judges, photographers, and fans. For the next 3 decades, Dora traveled through Africa and Europe looking for good waves—a calling most surfers would consider to be higher than that of a well-paid, full-time competitor.

Still, defenders of pro surfing have a strong case, starting with the biological fact that a young surfer's competitive drive will usually roll like a Panzer tank over the sport's more delicate and soulful interpretations. Kids will always test themselves against other kids. Abstinence from surfing competition would, in that sense, be unnatural. Also, most competitive surfers aren't defined by their lives in the arena. Two-time world champion Tom Carroll, for example, can move smoothly from competitor to big-wave rider to longboarder to world traveler. Furthermore—even with bad pro events as the standard—equipment, community, technique, and performance have all been advanced by competition. Finally, there is a short but admirable list of contests that, along with the Masters, have been virtually critic-proof.

What was missing all along was a new, custom-built format that would encourage and nurture those contests that put a premium on good surf. That change was in the works by early 1995. After two previous seasons—1993 and 1994—had been filled with intensely boring contests, there had been a near-mutinous reaction among world tour competitors and the surfing press. The world tour responded by hiring a new executive director, and the surf magazines, instead of simply trashing the whole enterprise, offered constructive

The 1986 Op Pro at Huntington Beach Pier in Orange County, California, was a classic "stadium event" surf contest—a concept that was fully realized for the first time at the inaugural Op Pro in 1982. The general idea was to hold the contest on a holiday weekend, create the greatest possible spectacle, and try to attract as many people as possible to the beach. Surfing conditions were a secondary consideration. The U.S. Open of Surfing, also held at Huntington Beach, has carried this bigger-is-better theme into the mid-1990s.

WORLD CHAMPIONS OF SURFING 1964-1996

BERNARD "MIDGET" FARRELLY, AUSTRALIA 1964

PHYLLIS O'DONNELL, AUSTRALIA 1964

FILIPE POMAR, PERU 1965

NAT YOUNG, AUSTRALIA 1966

JOYCE HOFFMAN, CALIFORNIA 1966

FRED HEMMINGS, HAWAII 1968

MARGO GODFREY OBERG, CALIFORNIA, HAWAII 1968, 1977, 1980, 1981

ROLF AURNESS, CALIFORNIA 1970

SHARON WEBER, HAWAII 1970, 1972

JIM BLEARS, HAWAII 1972

PETER TOWNEND, AUSTRALIA 1976

SHAUN TOMSON, SOUTH AFRICA 1977

WAYNE BARTHOLOMEW, AUSTRALIA 1978

LYNNE BOYER, HAWAII 1978, 1979

MARK RICHARDS, AUSTRALIA 1979, 1980, 1981, 1982

DEBBIE BEACHAM, CALIFORNIA 1982

TOM CARROLL, AUSTRALIA
1983, 1984

KIM MERIG, CALIFORNIA
1983

FRIEDA ZAMBA, FLORIDA
1984, 1985, 1986, 1988

TOM CURREN, CALIFORNIA
1985, 1986, 1990

DAMIEN HARDMAN
AUSTRALIA 1987, 1991

WENDY BOTHA, SOUTH AFRICA
1987, 1989, 1991, 1992

BARTON LYNCH, AUSTRALIA
1988

MARTIN POTTER,
SOUTH AFRICA 1989

PAM BURRIDGE, AUSTRALIA
1990

KELLY SLATER, FLORIDA
1992, 1994, 1995, 1996

DEREK HO, HAWAII
1993

PAULINE MENCZER,
AUSTRALIA 1993

LISA ANDERSEN, FLORIDA
1994, 1995, 1996

(NOTE: FROM 1964–1972 CHAMPIONS DECIDED IN A SINGLE EVENT; FROM 1976–1996 CHAMPIONS DECIDED BY THE WORLD TOUR.)

criticism. Most important, a half-dozen sponsors, working independently of each other, all at once embraced the good-waves-first principal. They would all give up on the minute-to-minute scheduling, the Sunday after-noon final, and the spectators on the beach. They would all go to the right location and put the show on hold until the good surf arrived. Five such events were scheduled in the middle of the 1995 season, and each was a smashing success. Perfect waves followed the pros around like a halo from South Africa to the South Pacific, Indonesia, Western Australia, and beyond. The shift wasn't complete—and, in fact, may never be. At least six of the overblown, stadium-style contests had all but welded themselves to the world tour schedule. But the time, energy, and expense that had gone into the new-look events had returned dividends not just in rousing performances in the water, but in red-hot film and video footage and stacks of print coverage. World tour offi-cials, to their credit, didn't overplay their PR hand. "We have just completed a year," wrote the new executive director, Graham Stapelberg, in review, "that has restored the credibility of this association." Never mind that "restored" was a dishonest choice of verbs. Stapelberg was on the right track. So, at last, was the world tour.

Confidence in surfing was high, and by early 1995, so were the dollars at stake. Surfing's com-mercial engine is fueled for the most part by a tight cluster of Southern California–based beachwear manufac-turers. Revenues were up in 1994 and were predicted to go higher in 1995 and beyond. As a result, world tour pro surfers—all of them smart enough to know that their salaries correspond almost directly to their year-end rating, and most of them acutely market-sensitive after the walloping surf industry crash of 1991—knew that 1995 would be a good time to post some big contest results.

Ten-year pro Sunny Garcia won the first event of the 1995 season, Machado won the second, and Slater the third. For the rest of the year there was little doubt that these surfers, in one configuration or another, would fill the top three spots at the end of the tour. Each would then sign a rich new contract: Machado's deal with Gotcha, and Garcia's agreement with No Fear, were both worth about $900,000 over 3 years. Slater's annu-al salary with Quiksilver was estimated to be a million dollars.

The three surfers were well-balanced geographically: Slater from Florida, Garcia from Hawaii, Machado from California. The same couldn't be said for their personal relationships. Garcia, raised in a tough neighborhood on the arid west side of Oahu, dropped out of high school at age 15. With his pitbulls, his tattooed back, and his death-ray stare, he'd long been portrayed as a thug and a recluse. He didn't often visit with Slater, but nonetheless liked and respected the world champion. Slater, in fact, was godfather to one of Garcia's children. Garcia for the most part ignored Machado, although he once went on record to discuss, with a slight but notable tone of disgust, Machado's

"For pure enjoyment and pure thrill," says 1977 world champion Shaun Tomson of South Africa (below), "tube riding comes first. Being spat out of one of those roaring, giant Hawaiian tubes is the most amazing sensation I've ever experienced. It's joy, fear, and accomplishment all rolled into one." Australian Tom Carroll (opposite page) won the world title in 1983 and 1984 and very nearly won it again on this particular morning at Pipeline in December 1988.

shortcomings in big surf. No real bitterness resulted. Garcia and Machado's relationship remained neutral.

Slater and Machado, meanwhile, shared the same manager. They were bandmates (about to record a CD for Epic) and golf partners. Both had graduated from high school with above-average marks—a rarity among their professional peers. Each was comfortable with his career station; Slater was the international sensation whose blurred expression—while running from his hotel room to the contest site a few steps ahead of his thronging fans—slightly resembled that of Paul McCartney at the height of Beatlemania. Machado, on the other hand, was the master of tranquillity, absorbing his measure of fame and fortune with quiet panache. Machado had defeated Slater in competition more often than any other surfer, but nonetheless accepted Slater as his generation's front man. Slater, meanwhile, trusted Machado not only as a friend from their pre-professional days, but as the surfer who best understood all facets, good and bad, of surf stardom.

Slater, Machado, and Garcia, before 1995, had already left their mark on the Pipe Masters event. Garcia surfed the finals of the 1992 Masters apparently perplexed from a wipeout that had sent him to the hospital with a torn muscle in his left forearm a few hours earlier. He then went headfirst into the rock bottom and wobbled off to a waiting ambulance asking, "What heat is it?" Garcia had performed well in each of his Masters starts but hadn't yet won.

Slater's luck had been better. After being shot like a cannonball from the mouth of a 10-foot Masters tube in 1991, the 19-year-old rookie had earned an instant big-wave standing to complement his invincible reputation in small waves, his rich endorsement contract, and his sparkling good looks (*People* magazine had just selected him as one of the year's 50 Most Beautiful People). He was pointed straight toward a world title in 1992. Slater's astonishing results at Pipeline over the next 3 years—two wins and a second—neatly measured the distance he'd put between himself and his peers. Nobody had ever surfed Pipeline with that kind of consistency and flair. Nobody had even come close.

Machado's first Masters start was in 1993. Like Slater, he entered as a dazzling small-wave surfer and future world title contender but without legitimizing North Shore credentials. "In Hawaii he's a zero," said *Surfer Magazine*, just as the 20-year-old Machado arrived on Oahu's North Shore for his first big-wave campaign as a professional. And at Pipeline in 1993, sure enough, Machado failed completely. In 8-to-10-foot surf he sat with visible trepidation in deep water off to the side, then seized up on his one and only big wave. It was an embarrassing performance and Machado fell back and reorganized.

By the middle of 1995, so had professional surfing. Although Slater won two of the good-surf-first pilot contests, surprising nobody, Machado's victory in Western Australia was something else completely. He'd seemingly gained precious little ground in his battle for big-wave respectability since the 1993 Masters. But in the long, hollow, and genuinely

Tom Curren is reflected in the first-place trophy he won in the 1987 Marui Open, held at Niijima, Japan. Curren's reputation as one of the greatest surfers in history is supported by his accomplishments as a competitor. But most surfers would define Curren first as an artist, then as a world champion. His smooth, flowing style was emulated by virtually every young surfer of the 1980s.

dangerous 8-foot lefts at a place called Gnaraloo, off a desolate stretch of Australian desert coast, he flowed his way to the top spot with the same offhand confidence that he had produced unfailingly in small-wave venues around the world.

Garcia didn't win any of the new contests, but his 1995 season was nonetheless the best of his magnificent career. Garcia was the last world title contender to have come of age professionally in the 1980s, and the difference showed in his surfing, which was deliberate, strong, elegant, and somewhat predictable. With effort, he was able to keep in check his contempt for the tail slides, reverses, aerials, and other slippery maneuvers favored by the younger set—"all those tricks" as Garcia put it. Because of his principled stand against the new style of surfing, he'd been written off by some as a contender for the 1995 world title. But in late November he was leading the ratings with only the Pipe Masters left on the schedule. Garcia sat back on his front porch overlooking Pipeline in the weeks leading up to the contest, with the Hawaiian grapevine buzzing about his awesome precontest form, and very much liked his chances. He had every reason to be confident. He'd been the top competitor in Hawaii for 3 years running. Slater, meanwhile, was so far behind on points that he could only be considered a long-shot contender ("In a way," Slater said just before the Masters, "I've already resigned myself to losing the title."), and Machado's surfing at Pipeline still had to be considered a work in progress. Garcia's prediction for the 1995 world tour finale was characteristically blunt. "Let me put it this way," he said, "if it were a horse race, I'd bet on me."

And with that swift kick to the ribs of fate, Garcia was done for. He fell apart completely in a second-round heat that should have been a walk in the park, and it was taken as gospel truth—even before Garcia marched stone-faced off the beach, bucked down from world champion to second runner-up—that the Hawaiian had arranged his own defeat through gross overconfidence.

With Garcia gone, attention shifted to Machado and Slater as they advanced steadily through the early rounds toward their inevitable semifinal match. Both surfers walled themselves off as the moment approached. The surf conditions, meanwhile, having already improved throughout the morning, now arranged in a silvery blend of wind, tide, sun, and ocean swell.

Slater and Machado paddled out. The opening horn sounded. A half-dozen waves were scored in the first 9 minutes, but none were significant. It was clear, however, that Machado had the greater task. Although he had a come a long way since 1993, he still hadn't reached Slater's level. Nevertheless, his just-burnished reputation as a cool man under pressure was holding up well. If it wasn't the huge, screaming, Freddy

The Quiksilver Surf Masters debuted in 1995 and was held in flawless conditions at G-Land on the island of Java. In contrast to the "stadium event" contests, the Surf Masters was held in a remote location, with virtually no audience on the beach. The object of this contest was simple: wait for good waves. This new approach was taken up by a few other sponsors at the same time, and pro surfing experienced a renaissance in the mid-1990s. Former world champion Derek Ho is shown here at the 1996 Surf Masters.

What is it about Florida that produces not just first-rate surfers, but habitual world champions? Lisa Andersen, shown here in Hawaii, and Kelly Slater each won titles in their respective divisions in 1994, 1995, and 1996. "Maybe," Andersen says, "Florida waves are so bad they just make world champions. Determined people live there, and you've got to have determination to win."

Krueger–style Pipeline surf that had graced previous Masters events, it was still the genuine article—strong enough to break surfboards and do bodily harm—and Machado, in earlier heats, had freely positioned himself deep in the vortex at every chance. Also, he had his opponent in a double-bind. Even if Slater won the semifinal, to take the world title from Machado, he'd still have to win the final heat against previous Masters winner Mark Occhilupo, the Brahma-built goofyfoot from Australia.

Ten minutes into the heat, Machado earned his perfect score, and Slater pulled off his extra-perfect response. With 20 minutes left, the match had essentially become a restart.

Two minutes later, Machado dropped into a set wave, pulled into the tube, traveled along for a few beats, then lost it, missing a 9-point-or-better opportunity.

One minute later he did the same thing.

Then Slater, as he'd done at fairly regular intervals throughout his career, seemingly began to surf outside the laws of gravity and drag. A cyclonic tube seemed to begin with a mistake, as Slater stalled his forward motion a moment too long while dropping down the face, then frantically increased his speed right before he disappeared from view. For 4 long seconds, the wave roared ahead, thick and opaque, and when Slater finally burst into daylight, 30 yards down the reef, he leaned back and flipped his hands palms-up—as if to say the whole thing was out of his control. Three minutes later he consolidated his position with a tube and immediately followed with another long disappearance. The performance and the speed of the exhibit were stunning. Slater had ridden three waves in just 5 minutes—during which time he not only vaulted past Machado, but made it clear that he would easily go on to defeat Occhilupo in the final that afternoon and win the world title.

But Machado nonetheless added a nice epilogue. Over the course of the semifinal's remaining 12 minutes, he came up with three excellent rides of his own, at one point flying out of a gorgeous powder-blue tube, cutting back slightly, and slapping palms with Slater, who was paddling back out. No way was Machado going to surpass his friend. But it was a good time for onlookers to take full measure of his classy presentation, along with that of the Masters and the entirety of the 1995 contest season. Slater was still off in the middle distance honing and refining the performance standard. But the competition and the forum itself were both moving up. 🏄

"I'm the most competitive person in the world," declares Kelly Slater. "Something in the way I was raised made me that way. Like I have to prove something all the time." While Slater is indeed a ravenous competitor, he generally has a good time in the process, and rarely has he felt better than during this ride (following spread) at the 1995 Chiemsee Pipe Masters.

REVOLUTION

LONGBOARDS, SHORTBOARDS, THRUSTERS, AND GUNS

Surfer/designer Bob McTavish was a general in the Australian-led shortboard revolution of the late 1960s. By the end of the decade, the average length of a surfboard had dropped from 10 to 6 feet, and surfers were finally able to race inside and around the curl instead of riding out in front of it as they had for 50 years. McTavish was short, stocky, and opinionated. This is why it is tempting to present him as the shortboard revolution's own Napoleon. But it can't be done. He's too friendly, too nice, and too relaxed.

McTavish worked like a fiend as a surfboard designer in the mid- and late 1960s. In 1967, he began to experiment with shorter, lighter, "vee-bottom" boards, which he hoped would allow greater planing speeds as well as a tighter turning radius. At the end of that year, he flew from Australia to the North Shore of Oahu, where, in the big surf of Sunset Beach, the vee-bottom failed spectacularly. But two weeks later, McTavish visited Honolua Bay, on the island of Maui, and this time his board worked just as he had hoped. It was, in fact, a high point in his life. The surf at Honolua was smooth and beautiful, and McTavish, at age 24, was at the top of his form. He was trading off waves with Nat Young—a good friend, an inspiring surfer, and former world champion. And, finally, the moment was being recorded and filmed for posterity.

That day on Maui was a triumph for McTavish. More significant, it was the symbolic moment of change between eras, from the classic longboard to the shortboard. Driving the change was the cultural, generational, and political hurricane that had fixed itself over surfing from 1966 to 1969—drawing energy from conflict and collaboration among drinkers, stoners, hippies, jocks, contest surfers, free surfers, corporate manufacturers, and backyard craftsmen. And all of *that* was just a reflection of what was taking place in the larger society. In the

late 1960s, a surfer couldn't step out of his front door without being spun around by the winds of change. And with enough fruits, vegetables, and brown rice, supplemented by yoga, pot, LSD, and the Kama Sutra, he could hope to duplicate internally the transformations taking place in the public domain. Minds were freed. Minds were fried. The vibrations were good except when punches were thrown.

In general, Bob McTavish moved through these turbulent years with balance and humor. He stayed clear of the fighting and he enjoyed the changes without giving himself over to them entirely. Above all else, he was a surfboard designer. While other surfers were doing similar

"I've always been a choppy, aggressive little surfer," says Australian surfer/ designer Bob McTavish. But on this day at Honolua Bay, in late 1967, McTavish, (left) riding a radical new board of his own making, was every bit the equal of 1966 world champion Nat Young (opposite page). An underwater view (previous spread) shows the mid-1990s surfboard in action.

Dewey Weber first tried surfing at age 9 on a 110-pound board made of redwood and pine. The year was 1947. It took 2 years before he successfully rode a wave. At 15, Weber opened his own surfboard shop. At 21 he starred in Bud Browne's 1959 surf movie, Cat on a Hot Foam Board, and by the mid-1960s, profits from Weber Surfboards had lifted Dewey to the fairly exclusive rank of "surfing millionaire."

work, none were more deeply involved than McTavish. He would, in later years, refer to himself as "just an old toymaker." But in his day, in his own way, he was on the front line of his culture and his sport.

Revolution happened just once in the first century of modern surfboard design. There were advances before and after, but nothing else had a similar impact. In the late 1920s, the blunt, solid, heavy, redwood plank, 10 feet in length, was surpassed in popularity by the lighter, longer (up to 16 feet), hollow "cigar box." This was in turn made obsolete by the streamlined, composite-wood "hot curl" boards of the 1930s. Developments just after World War II included a switch to lightweight balsa, the addition of a thin fiberglass shell along the surface of the entire board, and a rear-anchored stabilizing rudder, or "skeg." Polyurethane foam replaced wood as the core material in the late 1950s. But 10 feet remained the average surfboard length from the late 1930s to the late 1960s.

In Australia, surfboards in the mid-1950s still hadn't advanced past the cigar-box stage, since the country was almost completely cut off from the research and development taking place in Southern California and Hawaii. Change arrived in November 1956 when a team of American lifeguards arrived in Sydney to compete against the Australia life-saving clubs as an adjunct to the Melbourne Olympics. Some of the Americans brought along their lightweight balsa boards. They surfed up and down the east coast from Torquay to Avalon, then left their equipment behind to be used, studied, and copied. At that point, the Australian view of surfing was completely reordered. Hundreds of teenagers took to the ocean in what amounted to a loosely unified surfing crusade, and the country was quickly sponsored as a developing nation (along with France and Peru) in the surf world. America was soon exporting surf movies and magazines to Australia, and the balmy waves of New South Wales and Queensland began to attract overseas surfers. While Australian surfers were given to slavish imitation of the Americans, the first tender shoots of independence were seen in 1962, when 17-year-old Midget Farrelly, a Sydney surfer/board designer, entered and won the Makaha International, the biggest surf contest of the period.

When the American surfers visited Australia in 1956, Bob McTavish was 12 years old, living in central Queensland, and struggling with a leaky 16-foot hollow board. By the end of 1957, he had made himself an 8-foot balsa. Two years later he had his first foam board, and by 1963, after moving from Queensland to Sydney, he was getting paid to shape surfboards. McTavish surfed with an energetic, sometimes coarse style, but he was quick, and his maneuvering skills were on a level with Farrelly's. In November of that year, McTavish stowed away on a passenger ship to Hawaii. He spent 5 weeks there on the North Shore, developing a taste for big surf and a warming skepticism toward America's imperial role in the sport. "We were a little surprised at the level of surfing by many of the big [American] names," McTavish recalled years later. "In Australia, we'd have written them off as total eggrolls. Nice guys, but average surfers. Poor equipment, I felt, was a big part of this. I was ready to bow down to American board design, but quickly realized that these guys didn't have any great authority on what would or wouldn't work."

Australian confidence shot up in 1964 when Farrelly won the men's division of the inaugural world championships, held in Sydney. A good deal of attention was paid as well to local surfer Nat Young, an aggressive, loose-limbed 16-year-old and Farrelly disciple who finished runner-up in the junior division. Big things were predicted for Young.

Meanwhile, McTavish had moved back to Queensland, where he met George Greenough, a peculiar, solitary, round-shouldered surfer visiting from Santa Barbara. Greenough simply materialized one warm afternoon. He arrived barefoot, his Levi's held up by a length of rope, and he was carrying a one-of-a-kind, spoon-shaped, 4-foot, 8-inch balsa surfboard, with a long, swept-back skeg that he'd traced from the fin on a blue-fish tuna. McTavish was intrigued. He correctly marked Greenough as a genius and an eccentric. Not until the following morning, however, would he discover that this thin, almost spectral guest was also virtually amphibious. McTavish watched from the beach as Greenough kicked into a wave using swim fins, assumed a kneeling position on his tiny board, and ripped into a high-speed, sharply angled series of turns. In his mind, McTavish had already traced similar patterns on a wave; watching Greenough was like having his own imagination reflected back at him. He wondered how many years it would take before stand-up surfers could change direction on a wave the way Greenough did.

Greenough and McTavish got along famously and were soon portrayed in the Australian surf media as the sport's own Watson and Crick. The ascetic mad scientist from California was offset perfectly by the garrulous and friendly Australian—"A short, muscular guy," wrote a journalist in 1968, "with a battered puss and a wild, gold and paisley shirt. God knows how many times he's had his nose broken. McTavish himself forgets." Both were committed designers and builders. Neither had any real interest in organized competition. Greenough never entered a surf contest; McTavish, after finishing runner-up in the Australian titles in 1966, quit the circuit.

Nat Young, meanwhile, had become the hottest thing in surfing. In 1965, he broke away from Farrelly and joined forces with McTavish and Greenough. In 1966, at age 18, he entered the world championships in San Diego and won easily. The surfing public was then treated to a magnificent and long-running feud between Farrelly and Young.

The average surfboard in the mid-1960s was between 9 and 10 feet long and weighed 28 pounds. Surfers of the period could make relatively sharp changes in direction in small surf, but in bigger waves (below), they often did little more than angle for deep water. Hap Jacobs (opposite page)—shown here in 1960, working in his factory in Hermosa Beach, California—owned and operated Jacobs Surfboards, one of the 1960's most popular surf shops.

The two Australian world champions actually matched up in some fundamental areas. They were both national sports stars. They were both intelligent, verbal, self-centered, and able to march without distraction toward a goal. But everything compelling about the two lay in their differences. Farrelly's character is best introduced by the cold epigram he wrote for his 1967 book, *The Surfing Life:* "When you're comfortable, you're dead." His method in all things was structured, precise, polished, and analytical. A land-locked childhood in Canada and New Zealand meant that Farrelly hit the beach, at age 9, as an outsider, and he would always reside on the boundaries of surfing society. As a 19-year-old world champion in 1964, he carried himself like a middle-aged man. He valued privacy and moderation at an age when his contemporaries would gather by the dozen to drink and party until they passed out together in a heap. Farrelly's surfing, meanwhile, was smooth and crafted to a point where it looked risk-free. In truth, he was constantly defining and redefining his range, but the labor was hidden behind his competence.

Nat Young, meanwhile, walked the world surfing stage from the mid-1960s to the early 1970s like Louis XIV, running more on emotion than calculation. His feet, hands, and head were enormous, and at 6 feet, 3 inches, and 185 pounds, he could diminish Farrelly (no secret meaning to the nickname "Midget") just by standing next to him. Young was nicknamed "The Animal," and he loved it. His surfing was founded on power, and he brought power to bear in all his surf-world dealings. In 1966, he allegedly began a low-intensity campaign to encourage the idea that Farrelly's time as a great surfer had come and gone. An issue of Australia's *Surfing World* magazine from that year ran a full-page portrait of Farrelly next to an enormous headline: "An End to an Era?" Text elsewhere in the issue seems to answer the question: "Farrelly has been swept from the scene. What was good in 1964 is peanuts now." Young, McTavish, and Greenough all receive steady praise throughout the issue. A course was set for the next few years. Farrelly was the world title runner-up in 1968 and 1970 (beating Young both times), then had to stand back as reporters rushed over to ask Young why he didn't win.

As a surfer, Farrelly fought and lost his battle with Nat Young. As a board designer, he had similar luck with Bob McTavish.

In early 1967, McTavish once again moved to Sydney, and he and Farrelly were shaping surfboards about 20 miles from each other. The trend was toward faster, sharper turns, but nobody was yet willing to give away the stability that allowed surfers to walk forward and ride the nose of the board. As an action and an expression, the Americans had turned "hanging ten" into surfing's ultimate statement. Meanwhile, while the Australians were still pledging fealty to the Americans, the lord-vassal relationship was about to change—along with the surfboard itself.

As demonstrated to perfection in this photo (opposite page), surfboards designed and built for the Pipeline in Hawaii should do one thing above all else: cleave neatly down the face. If the board loses friction at this point, the surfer will be pitched into a dangerous wipeout. Australian surfer Terry Fitzgerald (below) is hypnotized by his mid-1970s "quiver" of surfboards, each built to match different aquatic terrain. Surfboards, in this respect, are like golf clubs.

"We were taking all of our cues from California," McTavish says today; "*Surfer Magazine*, Mickey Dora, and *The Endless Summer*—and a lot of nose riding. For 10 years, it had been that way. So it was very hard to saw the nose off a board and say, 'All right, we're not going to ride up there anymore.' Because it wasn't just saying good-bye to nose riding, it was saying good-bye to almost everything we knew about surfing; everything we'd learned from the Americans."

But McTavish knew that the nose-riders had literally and figuratively hit the end of the line. As he saw it, the energy source near the curl, an area known as "the pocket," was being terribly underutilized. The nose-riders were generally performing a few yards ahead of the breaking wave. This was understandable, McTavish recognized, since the 10-foot surfboard simply wouldn't react quickly enough to take a surfer up, down, around, through, and inside the curl—the way George Greenough was surfing. Greenough, of course, rode from a kneeling position and used swim-fins to propel himself into the waves. McTavish wanted to cover distance as his friend did, but he had to paddle, not kick, into waves, and ride in a stand-up position. It was an enormous design problem.

At first, McTavish built an elongated version of Greenough's kneeboard. It didn't work. Then in March of 1967, he made himself a 9-foot board with a longitudinal vee-shaped hull along the rear section that he hoped would destabilize the board into quicker turns. Energized by the peculiar look of his new vehicle, he painted "Plastic Machine" in huge, psychedelic letters along the bottom. The following morning, in well-shaped 3-foot surf, McTavish caught the day's first wave. He got to his feet, turned, and realized at once that the new board would perform just as he'd imagined. He stayed in the water for 9 straight hours. Two days later, he was back with an 8-foot, 6-inch Plastic Machine. One week after that, he made an 8-foot version. From May to September, McTavish designed, built and tested dozens of new boards, and even though he turned down a few blind alleys, the performance curve in general simply exploded. Board length, for the moment, bottomed out at 7 feet, 6 inches. The weight was reduced from 20 to 12 pounds. McTavish was now able to ricochet off the top of the wave, turn back into the whitewater, and put himself inside the curl.

Farrelly, meanwhile, working independently, was testing his own equipment along the same stretch of beach. The height and weight of his boards were similar to those McTavish was riding. The new maneuvers were all beautifully folded into Farrelly's style of surfing. But while his peers clamored for attention, Farrelly, for the most part, kept quiet and sent his boards to market without fanfare—which meant that his considerable involvement was all but ignored. *Surfer Magazine's* 9-page article introducing America to the shortboard never mentioned Farrelly's name. Nat Young, in his book, *The History of Surfing*, simply left Farrelly out of the narration from 1966 onward.

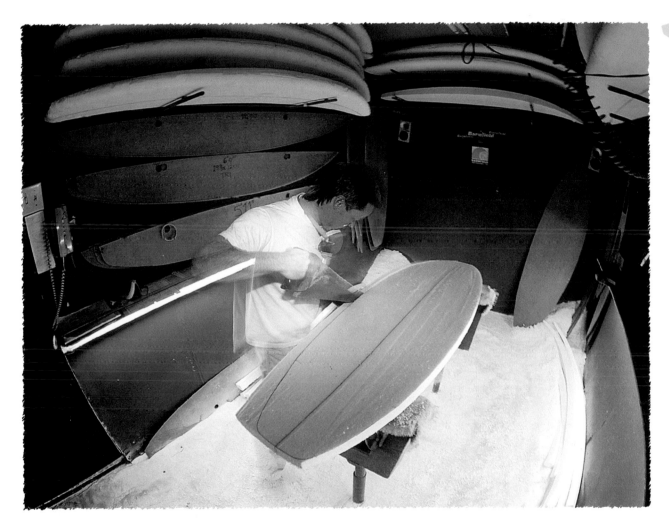

The shaper (left), alone among his surfboard manufacturing peers, is given credit as an artisan and designer. Kelly Slater rides a 6-pound surfboard (opposite page). Weight is a trade-off in surfboard design. Heavy boards are stronger but less responsive. Light boards perform better, but they're fragile. Slater, of course, opts for performance and is capable of thoroughly destroying up to 20 boards a year.

Over the years, the changing surfboard shapes have had an enormous impact on performance. So, too, has weight. Since the early part of the 20th century, average board weight has dropped from about 80 pounds to 6 pounds.

CIRCA 1975

CIRCA 1959

CIRCA 1930

CIRCA 1964

CIRCA 1995

CIRCA 1993

CIRCA 1979

CIRCA 1995

Due credit and recognition aside, the short surfboard, by November 1967, had been road tested thoroughly and declared sound for small-wave use. Now came December and the annual big-wave congregation on the North Shore of Oahu. For more than 20 years the North Shore had been surfing's final proving grounds. This season, it loomed like a brick wall—not just for the new boards, but for the new thinking in general. Members of the old guard were smirking and rubbing one callused hand over the other—and they seemed to have just cause. Procedural rules in Hawaii wouldn't be easily changed. Big waves meant big boards and dead-ahead surfing. A surfer paddling a skittish vee-bottom surfboard into a roaring 20-foot wave at Sunset Beach or Waimea Bay might easily suffer a complete ideological breakdown, dropping all thoughts of "self-expression" and "total involvement" for a wide-splayed survival stance and a prayer for raw forward motion.

Bob McTavish had more confidence than that. Nonetheless, the vee-bottom board he made himself for the Duke contest in Hawaii was back up to 9 feet. Radical, he thought, but not ridiculous.

The Duke Kahanamoku Surfing Classic, held at Sunset Beach, debuted 2 years earlier and had instantly become surfing's most prestigious event. The once-mighty Makaha International contest, held on the west side of Oahu, was now viewed as a relic. The U.S. Championships at Orange County's Huntington Beach Pier took place each summer in chronically poor surf. But in 1967, the integrity of the Duke was also in question. Contest officials had drawn up and circulated a roster of 24 invited surfers, and it was hard to look at the list of names and not see a number of political vendettas and favors being played out. McTavish, never an avid competitor, made the cut. World champions Farrelly and Young didn't.

On the morning of the contest, December 15, McTavish had to drive across the island to the Honolulu Airport to pick up his board, which had been lost in transit from Australia a few days earlier. Back on the beach at Sunset, he glanced out at the agitated 10-foot surf, then was sent immediately into his first-round match. What happened in the next 40 minutes was subject to debate. McTavish without question produced a great assortment of wipeouts and spent much of his allotted time swimming after his board on his way to a nonadvancing finish. The question was whether or not McTavish did anything interesting in the moments before falling off. *Surfer* thought so: "Using an experimental 9-foot board with a thick vee-bottom tail," the magazine wrote, "McTavish demonstrated that he's one of the most creative surfers in the sport. His wipeouts came mostly from just being unfamiliar with the heavy-toppling Sunset peaks." Midget Farrelly didn't see it that way. "The boards that worked so well in Sydney," he said, "were now [in Hawaii] impotent pieces of foam and glass."

McTavish knew the vee-bottom had failed at Sunset. The

Riding on the pared-down surfboards of the early 1990s, surfers had to push constantly or risk losing forward thrust. The quick, steep, hollow waves at Off the Wall and Backdoor Pipeline, in Hawaii, are perfect for this type of equipment, allowing riders like California's Matt Archbold (opposite page) to cover more area in a shorter period of time than ever before. The three-fin surfboard (below) has been the industry standard since the early 1980s.

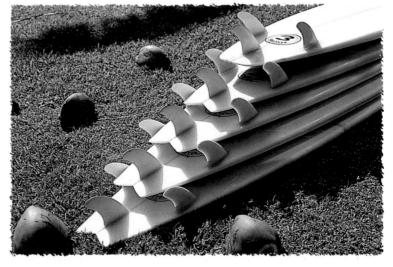

Duke experience, in fact, put a check on what had been a fairly steady 10-month march. McTavish was contemplative, if not quite thoroughly discouraged, as he joined up with Nat Young and boarded a plane for the 25-minute flight to Maui and Honolua Bay.

Australian surfer Simon Anderson debuted the three-fin surfboard in 1981, and board design for the rest of the decade was for the most part limited to a series of refinements of Anderson's original model. In the 1990s, however, creative new work has been done on the revived longboard, as well as the wide-backed shortboard (below) and the miniature board for big-wave use (opposite page).

McTavish stood up on his first wave at Honolua and leaned to his right. The tail section of his board lost contact with the face of the wave and slipped downward, and for an instant it looked as if McTavish would fall off. Another swim. Another setback. But with a quick shift of weight McTavish reset the rail, trimmed along for a few yards, then made a quick exit. Hardly revolutionary, but at least he'd kept it together.

The afternoon built steadily from there. The surf was about the same height Sunset had been for the Duke contest. But where Sunset was knotted and disorderly, the surf at Honolua was taut, refined, and smooth. Later in the day, the sun began to shine through the backs of the waves, turning them emerald green. The critics were elsewhere. Nat Young, on a vee-bottom board almost identical to McTavish's, was an inspiration.

On his second wave, McTavish widened his stance by a few inches, settled his feet into the deck of his board, and felt a sense of control returning. The vee-bottom's high-strung handling characteristics, he knew, could be worked through. Minutes later, on another wave, he drove high across the pocket, released downward, turned off the bottom and again banked high along the wall, racing the curl. The loose, unrestricted feeling that he'd grown accustomed to along the Sydney beaches now rushed back. Paddling back out, McTavish saw Young on the next wave ranging easily from the trough to the crest, and the Honolua event was now almost stereophonic.

Australian filmmaker Paul Witzig, meanwhile, was stationed behind his camera on the cliff overlooking the bay. Within two months the footage Witzig shot would be seen in beach towns in California, Hawaii, and Australia as the closing sequence to his new film, *The Hot Generation*. John Witzig, Paul's brother and a *Surfer Magazine* correspondent, was also at Honolua. "If you see the surfing of Nat and McTavish," Witzig wrote in his upcoming article, "your ideas of surfing can never be the same."

In revolutionary terms, it was a complete triumph. The classic longboard had been rendered obsolete, and the idea of surfing inside and around the curl—instead of out in front of it—would from that point forward be a prerequisite to high-performance surfing.

McTavish would always recognize his place at the middle of the shortboard campaign. "Here's a guy," he said recently, summing up a youthful version of himself, "who can lead a bit of a charge." But at the end of 1967, still buzzing on the memory of a Honolua tube-ride, McTavish metaphorically reached for a church setting, rather than a battlefield. He recalled a blue-green Hawaiian curl slicing through the air over his head. "Coming over!" he wrote. "Right over! Inside! A GIANT GREEN CATHEDRAL, AND I AM THERE!"

THE
UNRIDDEN
REALM

Pat Curren rode an enormous wave at Hawaii's Waimea Bay in early 1960, with cameras on the beach following his progress, and a few weeks later the ride turned up as a fine dramatic ending to Bruce Brown's new film, *Surf Crazy*. The shot still has energy. A burlesque rock and roll instrumental is driving the *Surf Crazy* soundtrack as Curren, the near-mute Waimea savant, begins his ride, using a streamlined balsa board of his own design and flanked by two other surfers. Big-wave surfing was still new and rough, and the three surfers here look like delinquent teenagers jumping off a bridge as they charge down the face of the wave. Brown, the narrator, almost can't take the excitement. "Then the biggest wave in the past 5 years! Maybe the biggest wave ever ridden! Peter Cole, Byron Cough, Pat Curren! Watch the size of it!" Brown pauses as the surfers on either side of Curren get annihilated, then goes a half-octave higher to drive home the obvious point. "And Pat Curren makes it!"

Curren's wave, the biggest ridden in 1960, measured about 25 feet. (A big wave, for the moment, can be defined at over 20 feet). In 1996, Laird Hamilton caught the biggest wave of the year—a 35-footer. A 10-foot addition after 36 years doesn't seem like much. The fact that a full three-quarters of the height jump was made from 1993 to 1996, however, is nothing less than amazing.

Before the early 1990s, the basic parameters of big-wave surfing had remained virtually unchanged for decades. All big-wave riders moved through the surf zone under their own power. The big-wave solar system revolved around Waimea Bay as surely as the planets revolve around the sun. And the frontier of the big-wave experience ended just past 25 feet—beyond which, as characterized in the mid-1980s by surfer and dramatist Mark Foo, lay "the unridden realm."

The 25-foot "limit," of course, has little to do with the actual height of a really big wave. A photograph from the 1990 Quiksilver contest, showing Brock Little in an awful moment of weightlessness—just as his feet lose contact with the deck of his surfboard—clearly makes the point. The wave he's riding is really a 40-footer, but it was described as 25 feet, which says something about the big-wave franchise. The difference between real and stated wave size is in small part a matter of science. (Oceanographers measure the low-to-the-surface offshore ocean swell, not the fully-expanded breaking wave—exactly why this has any significance to surfers is unknown.) But the bigger reason for the downgrading has to

Californians Mickey Muñoz and Mike Stange learn big-wave surfing by trial and error. "Waimea was a real taboo deal," recalls Greg Noll. "People thought if you wiped out you'd die. Then we finally went out there and did it. The ocean didn't swallow us up, and the world didn't stop turning." Waimea surfers Peter Cole and Buzzy Trent (opposite page) bring science to the deep-water wipeout. Laird Hamilton (previous spread) at Jaws, in Maui, February 6, 1996.

do with Hawaiian-style machismo, in which studied nonchalance indicates mastery. Wave heights were minimized throughout the 1970s, and by the mid-1980s a big-wave sage might raise a casual eyebrow out toward a furious set of two-story billows at Sunset Beach and calmly identify them as 8-footers, as if he'd just measured off a length of drywall.

While the 25-foot measurement has often been unreal, the boundary it signifies is genuine. With all the elements in perfect synch, a surfer can paddle into a 25-foot wave, get to his feet just as the crest pitches forward, overcome the tremendous base-to-apex rush of water, and drive down and across for a completed ride. At 30 feet, it can't be done. As demonstrated in a small but telling number of film and video clips, a surfer will usually come undone on a 30-foot wave in one of two ways. He'll make short progress down the face, stall as the water velocity pulls against him, then get sucked back up the precipice. Or, if forward thrust is maintained, he'll quickly hit a speed (at about 30 or 35 miles per hour) that voids all control mechanisms on his board.

Most of the problem has to do with equipment. The big-wave surfboard has traditionally been faulty in two related areas: it's too slow on entry (the takeoff), and too fast during the ride itself. The first, obviously, is more important. You have to *catch* a big wave before you can ride it. High paddling speed, therefore, has always been a standard design feature, which means that the specialized big-wave board through the decades has been long, thick, and streamlined. Called an "elephant gun" or "rhino chaser" in the late 1950s and 1960s, today's "gun" is roughly 10 feet long, 20 inches wide, 3 1/2 inches thick, and weighs between 25 and 30 pounds. Once fully engaged on the wave face, however, the best gun in the world will stretch out in front of a surfer like a flatbed railway car, too big to control with any efficiency. "I don't like boards over 9 feet, 8 inches," Little told *Surfing* magazine in 1996, "because they ride me, I don't ride them."

The problem is fundamental, as well as confounding, which is why Pat Curren, as the first full-time big-wave board specialist, virtually exhausted the design possibilities. It was equipment deficiency, not lack of courage or technique, that prevented Curren from riding a wave significantly bigger than the one he caught in 1960. Following generations of big-wave board designers made only slight improvements.

Then everything changed in 1992. Maverick's altered the rotation of the big-wave world, and tow-in surfing put it into an entirely new orbit.

Maverick's, an oppressive Northern California break, made the greater first impression on the surfing public. Hidden in plain sight between San Francisco and Santa Cruz, Maverick's for 15 years, had been a virtual one-man province for Half Moon Bay surfer Jeff Clark, who knew from the beginning that his spot, in ways both thrilling and terrible,

Australian pro surfer Ian Cairns (opposite page) follows an unidentified rider at Waimea Bay during the 1975 Smirnoff competition. Cairns finished the day in second place, and won $2,000. (Below) The warm water and tropical setting of Waimea can have a soothing effect on what is, for most surfers, an event made up of equal parts terror and exhilaration. This unusual outside-looking-in perspective was photographed in 1966.

matched up evenly against Waimea Bay. Since 1975, Clark had surfed Maverick's alone. Meanwhile, in the late 1980s, 500 miles to the south, 20-foot-plus surf was being ridden at a newly discovered Mexican break called Todos Santos. This meant that the collective big-wave consciousness had already branched out across the Pacific by the time Clark began inviting surfers and photographers to Half Moon Bay in 1992. But none of Clark's visitors were really prepared for what they found at Maverick's. Photojournalists captured a 25-foot wave Richard Schmidt rode at Maverick's in January of 1992, and it lay on the pages of the surf magazines like photographic proof of alien life. The shock was tremendous. Schmidt's wave was big, shaded in ominous blue-black tones (big surf waves in Hawaii are much prettier than those in California), and it seemed to contain half the weight of the Pacific Ocean. The Hawaiian big-wave collective was smashed. For the first time, big-wave surfers began to leave Hawaii, at least for a few days at a time, and head to Maverick's during the winter months.

Hawaii's big-wave impresario, Mark Foo, had already made a half-dozen migratory visits to Todos Santos, and by the end of 1994 he was fixed on the prospect of surfing Maverick's. Foo, by this time had spent 10 years in the first rank of big-wave surfers. He had given himself over completely to his specialized career, which he embraced not just as a discipline, a calling, and an art form, but as a business—which meant he was ready at all times to follow the winds of change. He drove away from his well-appointed house at Waimea Bay on the evening of December 22 and boarded a red-eye flight for San Francisco, looking as always for big surf and publicity. He'd been looking for a reason to use an open-date round-trip ticket that he'd been holding for nearly a year, and this seemed like the right moment. Everyone in surfing knew Maverick's would be a big newsmaker in the months ahead. The surf had been consistently big since early December, and photographers, filmmakers, and journalists were all on call. In this convergence of events, Foo would have seen evidence of his "special destiny"—a phrase he often used.

But at Maverick's, it was Foo's destiny and plain bad luck to die after wiping out on a 15-foot wave, six hours after arriving in San Francisco. Surfing's great overachiever had truly outdone himself. Foo temporarily became the most famous surfer in the world and modern surfing's first big-wave martyr.

Journalists from *The New York Times*, *Paris Match*, *Rolling Stone*, *Spin*, MTV, and NBC's *Dateline* all worked hard to create a proper context for Foo's death, detailing the big-wave surfing subculture's history, equipment, geography, and philosophy. Some did a better job than others. But none caught on to the fact that they were describing a form of big-wave surfing that had already peaked. The tow-in surfers, back in Hawaii, were about to put themselves deeply and smoothly into the unridden realm that Foo had so often talked about and had never reached.

Hawaiian surfer Brock Little (below), just before a wipeout during the 1990 Quiksilver contest at Waimea. Little knows how to play up the drama. "I'm totaly stoked if I get into a radical experience. I don't mind being held underwater. I don't mind bleeding. I've walked away from everything that's happened so far and been better off every time." (Opposite page) Contestants line up for the Quiksilver contest opening ceremony in 1988.

This oversized wave at Todos Santos (previous spread) was produced by the same north Pacific storm that generated the Waimea wave on page 98. Mark Foo (below) at Todos Santos in 1992. December 23, 1994: this Maverick's wave (opposite page) overtook both Mike Parsons and Brock Little. Unbeknownst to both, Hawaiian surfer Mark Foo had wiped out on the previous wave and was underwater nearby, about to lose his life. The dangers of big-wave surfing, once thought to be exaggerated, are now being reconsidered.

Two years earlier, at the end of 1992—while Jeff Clark stood at the gates of his big-wave asylum in Half Moon Bay and waved in the new arrivals—Laird Hamilton, Darrick Doerner, and Buzzy Kerbox loaded their boards one afternoon into a 60-horsepower Zodiac inflatable boat and buzzed through the channel to the outlying reefs of Backyards, just east of Oahu's Sunset Beach. The surf was about 15 feet. Again and again, the view from a distance was the same: two surfers sitting in the boat and circling around, perhaps a half-mile beyond the breaking waves, while the third surfer, already standing on his board, trailed behind holding on to a 30-foot length of water ski rope. When a likely swell moved in, the rider gave a signal, and the boat aimed toward shore, just ahead of the building wave. When the wave tilted up steeply enough for the surfer to ride unassisted, he dropped the rope and maintained—or actually increased—velocity with two or three long, sweeping turns, as the boat peeled off toward deep water. Perhaps 75 yards after dropping the rope, with the wave now about to spill over—at a point where a paddling surfer might be pushing to his feet from a virtual cold start and hoping for the best—the tow-in surfer was in overdrive and perfectly balanced. From here the ride proceeded more or less as it would if the surfer had paddled into the wave. Seconds later, in the deep water of an adjoining channel, he reconnected with the boat, everyone traded places, and the whole procedure was repeated.

A handful of surfers, in the weeks that followed, recognized that the Backyards session was only a small demonstration project and that Hamilton and his friends were preparing for what amounted to a big-wave space shot. Thousands of others, however, took one look at the new procedure and were put off. On a gut level, using the boat to tow them meant these guys were *cheating*. On another level, they were stretching or breaking esthetic laws. Surfers regularly find peace, beauty, solitude, even God, in the ocean. Nonmechanization is considered a precondition to such feelings of calm and equanimity. Hamilton and his friends, as many saw it, had done nothing less than run a Harley through the hanging gardens.

But the criticism never gained momentum. It helped that the tow-in riders were so highly placed in the surfing world. Kerbox was a top-rated pro in the late 1970s. Doerner was perhaps the most respected big-wave surfer in the world, and Hamilton, the youngest at age 28, was seen as a big-wave rider of almost limitless potential. More important was the realization that tow-in surfing simply wasn't going to directly interfere in the least with anyone's surfing life. In a very small way, this was due to coastal laws barring the use of "personal watercraft" in the surf zone. Far more important was the idea that perhaps just six dozen surfers in the world have the money, desire, and ability, not to mention proximity to suitable waves, to even *begin* thinking about tow-in surfing. It simply doesn't exist for anyone else, except in magazines and videotapes.

Now pacified, the general surf community soon came to acknowledge both the logic and visceral thrill of tow-in surfing. The natural greediness of most surfers, for example, led them to appreciate the sheer number of big waves now on offer. As Doerner said in the spring of 1993, "I caught more big waves last winter than probably the last 10 years combined." Hamilton, when fully pumped up, can squeeze in an amazing 20 waves per hour.

Finally, and most important, it was now obvious to big-wave spectators, as well as big-wave surfers, that the long-standing 25-foot boundary would be driven, not paddled, around.

After their introduction at Backyards in 1992, the tow-in surfers regularly left the surf world dumbfounded. In late 1993, Hamilton was riding 25-foot-plus surf, his feet now strapped to the deck of his board, drawing lines across the huge faces as easily as if he were finger painting. Later in the year, Hamilton's performance in Bruce Brown's *Endless Summer II* delivered the greatest secondhand big-wave rush since Pat Curren's Waimea drop from *Surf Crazy*. On December 20, 1994, 3 days before Mark Foo died at Maverick's, tow-in surfer David Kalama was photographed on a wave that might have been 10 feet bigger than any wave yet ridden. On November 23, 1995, Hamilton bettered Kamala's mark. *Surfing* magazine called Hamilton's wave "frankly unbelievable" and estimated the face at 60 feet. (The face, of course, is never offered by surfers or the surf media as a serious measurement of wave height. By late 1996, the surf magazines finally determined that Hamilton had set the new mark at 35 feet.)

Meanwhile, the tow-in enterprise had further widened the gap between big-wave surfing and mainstream surfing. The core tow-in group was filled out by a handful of wave-riding sailboarders—Hamilton himself is a former speed-sailing champion—and the main operation was now headquartered on the north shore of Maui, near a roaring big-wave break appropriately called "Jaws." (Having already suffered the indignation of Maverick's, Waimea's status throughout the mid-1990s was in freefall. The Quiksilver big-wave contest scheduled for Waimea in 1995 was called off due to lack of surf. Then *Surfing* magazine, in early 1996, all but penned the spot's epitaph: "More and more surfers are discovering the dirty secret behind the Bay: if you've got a big modern gun and even an ounce of attitude, it's really not that hard to ride.")

The atmosphere around the Maui tow-in surfers had a vaguely mercenary smell. Almost immediately, the group put together a film company and a surfing equipment product line, hoping to turn a profit from their big-wave adventures. Still, they were producing an impressive amount of pure research and development. The Zodiac boats were quickly retired in favor of Jet Skis—mostly two-stroke, 650cc Yamaha WaveRunners. And,

Surf photography at Maverick's is often done from the deck of a fishing boat (below). Jay Moriarity at Maverick's (opposite page), in December 1994, about to launch into one of surf history's most spectacular wipeouts. A few weeks later, the 16-year-old Moriarity said: "From what I've learned about wiping out, you just have to relax and let it beat the crap out of you and hope you come up. So I relaxed."

because the paddling requirement was completely lifted, designers of big-wave surfboards for the first time ever were allowed a totally clean slate. The first order of business was to take an age-old principal—bigger boards for bigger waves—and turn it upside down. The point now was to *surf* big waves, not catch them. High speeds demand less board volume. Almost immediately, the bow-to-stern measurement was reduced by 3 feet, and a corresponding amount was taken off the width. By early 1996, the biggest waves in the world were being ridden on boards 7 feet, 2 inches long, and 15 inches wide. Lead weights were fastened to the deck as ballast. Looking back to go forward, some of the new boards were made out of wood.

Laird Hamilton entered the tow-in project as first among equals and from 1992 to 1996 had done nothing but consolidate his leadership position. As the son of 1960s surf icon Bill Hamilton, Laird was brought up on the beach, among the world's best surfers, and as a strapping 3-year-old was up and riding on his own custom-built board. There was never any question that he would become an excellent surfer. Anyone taking a close enough look might also have said that Hamilton, with his ever-growing muscle mass and powers of concentration, would eventually come up with something—a stunt, a scam, maybe a career—that would blow minds on an international scale. But it took some time. Organized competition didn't interest him. Hamilton's size (6 feet, 3 inches, and 225 pounds) made him a nonstarter. That said, he probably owns the greatest combination of athletic gifts ever found in a surfer: intelligence in the water, courage, finesse, poise, and enormous strength. Power radiates almost visibly from his chest and biceps. His jawline appears to be underpinned with steel girders. But the most powerful thing about Hamilton, ultimately, is his undiluted, free-flowing intensity. It may be this quality, more than his looks, that seems to push other surfers out of focus when they step into his immediate range.

Tow-in surfing gave Hamilton a sense of purpose. He declared his full-time occupation in a 1994 magazine cover story: "Riding the Biggest Waves Ever." Greg Noll, in 1969, had set the reigning standard at 30 feet. As it turned out, the advantage of a Jet Ski was so great that breaking Noll's record involved little more than waiting for the right day of surf. If there was any doubt that Hamilton had equaled or bettered Noll's mark dur-

The biggest advantage tow-in surfers have over traditional big-wave surfers is found at the beginning of the ride. To illustrate, compare Laird Hamilton's high-speed, fully controlled takeoff at Jaws (previous spread), to Jay Moriarity's nowhere-to-go-but-down entry at Maverick's on page 105. (Below) Hamilton's flashy exit at Jaws.

ing the winter of 1994–95, his November wave of the following season—the one *Surfing* estimated at 60 feet on the face—put the matter to rest.

But tow-in surfing had been an advanced study in big-wave maneuverability and performance, as much as height. The project now became more complicated. Thinking about what it might take to set up a ride through one of Jaws's atom-smashing tubes, Hamilton sounded a rare note of caution: "We want to start riding in the barrel out there, but it's a whole new trip. Some of the waves stay open, but a lot of them don't. The bottom line is, we're not in any hurry."

Darrick Doerner, 8 years older than Hamilton, *was* in a hurry.

After their preliminary tow-in work together at Backyards in the winter of 1992–93, Doerner and Hamilton had moved on to separate tracks. Hamilton went to Maui, gathered together his sailboarding friends, and did virtually all of his tow-in surfing at Jaws. Doerner stayed on Oahu, formed a smaller, independent tow-in partnership with Buzzy Kerbox, and quietly began exploring a series of outer reefs along the North Shore. For 3 years, it often seemed as if Hamilton was the only tow-in surfer in Hawaii. Then on Thanksgiving Day 1995, Doerner dropped into an enormous, ultrasmooth wave at Outside Alligator Rock, located about 3 miles east of Backyards, and without hesitation trimmed up high into the tube. He was shut down, but not before he'd planted the new big-wave flag. Tube riding had long been seen as the next logical step for tow-in surfing. The surprise was that Doerner did it first.

It was early in the season. Doerner's ride was instant news in Maui, and Hamilton's muscles started twitching in response.

Ten weeks later, on February 6, 1996, Doerner flew to Maui and drove out into 30-foot-plus surf at Jaws, where he and Hamilton met in an unsmiling but gentlemanly big-wave face-off. Each surfer rode more than a dozen enormous waves, but the day was easily reducible to one spectacular exchange. Doerner was first up. He angled three-quarters of the way down what was likely the biggest wave of the afternoon, leaned carefully over his inside rail, then eased back up the face, spread his arms wide, and locked himself into a speed stance as the top of the wave formed a ragged cantilever well above his head. The wave folded over, and a shadow fell across Doerner as he crouched in the portals of a tube at least 10 feet bigger than the one he'd attempted on Thanksgiving. This wave was between 30 and 35 feet. And this time he made it.

Hamilton, by chance, was in the channel adjacent to the break and saw Doerner's wave from start to finish. He screamed to his Jet Ski driver, "Get me over there! *Deep!*" and moments later picked up a wave that was a shade under 30 feet. Hamilton's path across the face was similar to Doerner's, but, as requested, he'd started from further back, and for a long beat, as the curl pitched into space, then exploded along the base of the wave, he vanished completely from view. The wave was smaller than Doerner's, but Hamilton had placed himself further inside. Hamilton, like Doerner, then charged back into sight.

The two-wave suite lasted no more than 3 minutes. Doerner now had the *biggest* big-wave tube on record, Hamilton had the deepest, and chances were that neither mark would stand by the end of the following season. Stasis had for decades been the hallmark of big-wave surfing; now everything was fluidity and change. The seat of power was again back in Hawaii. The paddle-in era of maximum big-wave riding was over. Hamilton, Doerner, and a few others were operating in a big-wave domain that, for the moment, had only the sketchiest of boundaries. ♪

Buzzy Kerbox, Darrick Doerner, and Laird Hamilton (left to right) minutes before their first tow-in trial at Backyards in Hawaii. "We're just building up, figuring the whole thing out," Doerner said at the time, "because one day a 30-plus set's going to come in, and we're going to be ready for it."

(Following spread) Darrick Doerner at Jaws, January 6, 1996, in a matter of seconds reestablished the performance boundaries for big-wave surfing.

Surf culture had firmly infiltrated America's consciousness by 1964. In the March issue of *Surf Guide* magazine that year, a full-page ad announced that the Makaha Surf-Skateboard was now available at Broadway, the Emporium, and Macy's department stores. An upset *Surf Guide* reader sent in a letter complaining about an "obscene and offensive" photograph that had run in an earlier issue, showing young surfers on the beach dancing the Surfer's Stomp: "You certainly shouldn't print photos of half-clothed girls and cigarette-smoking ruffians!" A feature article titled "Surfing Goes Hollywood" noted with some ambivalence that *Beach Party*, American International Pictures' 1963 release, had earned a tidy $4 million, and that a sequel, *Muscle Beach Party*, was now in post-production. And finally, in the back section of the magazine, there was a short review of an event that had, in a single stroke, defined the accelerating Southern California beach craze: the Second Annual Los Angeles Surf Fair.

The Surf Fair had taken place at the Santa Monica Civic Auditorium, 20 minutes southeast of Malibu, on December 27 and 28, 1963. *Surf Guide* and radio station KRLA were co-sponsors. Events had included a bikini contest, a battle of the surf bands (headlined by the Surfaris and the Surf-Tones), and a festival of surf movies. Surfing, skateboarding, and skimboarding competitions were staged, along with a car show featuring a "hand-built, Rolls-Royce surf-wagon, complete with leopard skin upholstery." But the main action had taken place in the Civic Auditorium exhibitors' hall, where top surfboard manufacturers—along with a few dozen second-division board-builders, plus surf clubs, clothing companies, and makers of wetsuits, surf racks, surf books, and magazines—had set up display booths and settled in for a weekend of socializing and light work.

A few hundred surfers had filed through the Civic turnstiles on Surf Fair weekend, most of them dressed in Levi's and Keds, with white competition T-shirts underneath wool Pendletons. Their general mood wandered from indifference to somewhat stoked. They directed smirks toward the two kooks in ties and cardigan sweaters who sat at the Salt Creek Surfing Society booth, next to a sign that declared them "dedicated to the exchange of ideas in regard to the formation and mechanics of surfing clubs." On the other hand, nearly everyone thought the Jacobs Surfboards booth was totally boss. Surfer Mike Doyle wasn't actually there himself, but his board was, and glued to the middle of the board was a picture of Doyle on a heavy-duty Sunset Beach boomer. Rusty Miller's board was next to Doyle's, with a picture of Miller at the Pipeline. A lot of people had Doyle picked as the favorite for the upcoming world titles. Miller had made the finals of the West Coast championships the year

The Jacobs booth was a top atraction at the 1964 Surf Fair. Many surfers who came of age in the 1950s were offended by surfing's commercial growth in the early 1960s. "I'd grown up among the first full generation of Australian surfers," says 1964 world champion Midget Farrelly. "Then here comes the first commercial surfers, and suddenly I was in the middle of this cardboard Coca-Cola culture. Surfers all of a sudden were opportunistic. They wanted so much more than they had."

E "Everybody's gone surfin'/Surfin' USA": By the time the Beach Boys hit No. 3 on the Billboard charts in 1963 with "Surfin' USA," the beach scene at Malibu seemed to offer quantitative proof that everybody had indeed been caught up in this latest teen craze. Adding to the frenzy, Columbia Pictures released Beach Party, in 1963, the first (not counting Gidget) in a series of lightweight Hollywood movies starring Frankie Avalon and former Mouseketeer Annette Funicello.

before. No doubt, in the minds of most who streamed through the Civic, the Jacobs booth was bitchin', for sure.

The Greg Noll Surfboards display, however, was looking pretty weak. Tucked off the main thoroughfare, on the far side of the hall, the booth featured three surfboards, a few scattered boxes, a plain metal fold-out table and two fold-out chairs. A hand-lettered "Greg Noll Surfboards" banner was tacked to the wall, along with a pair of surf trunks and a droopy length of nylon fishing net. It was probably a 20-minute installation job. Nothing whatsoever to identify the presenter as one of the top 10 board-builders in the country.

Then the display strategy was made clear as Noll himself stepped into the 10-by-20-foot area. The surfboards, the banner, and the nylon net were all fluff. Noll was the exhibit, and suddenly the entire Surf Fair show seemed to tilt in his direction. This was partly due to his corporeal mass (at 6 feet, 2 inches, and 220 pounds, he was appropriately nicknamed "Da Bull") and partly to his untouchable North Shore reputation. He'd ridden the world's biggest waves. He'd been annihilated by the world's biggest waves, surfaced, grabbed his board, and paddled right back out.

Everything about Noll seemed heavy and grounded, yet in many ways he was the Surf Fair's most nimble exhibitor. As a businessman, he understood perfectly the link between a cleaned-up image for the sport and improved sales. As a frequent contributor to *Petersen's Surfing*, he had tacitly endorsed the magazine's credo, which read in part: "We respect the rights of the community and its members. Our conduct will set a mature and responsible example of the proper respect for people and property." A few weeks before the Surf Fair, Noll had stunt-doubled for James Mitchum in Columbia Pictures' upcoming *Ride the Wild Surf*, another surfing morality play from Hollywood in which hard work, education, and convention triumphed over recreation and idiosyncrasy.

But not by any stretch of the imagination could Noll be viewed as a paragon of surfing virtue. His greatest efforts had gone toward the invention of a surfing culture that combined drinking, brawling, and minor vandalism with great inventiveness in dress, language, and entertainment. Noll was a true representative of his sport, and he constantly walked the line between clever and idiotic. In the eighth grade, he once attended class in a trench coat with a rotting anchovy hidden in a side pocket—just to find out how long it would take him to get a reaction. He later painted swastikas on his car for the same reason. Noll's standing in surf history is a lesson in the importance of time and setting. In another town, in another era, he would have had his moment as the local smart-ass and vanished. Instead, today he's long been revered as an apostle of early surf culture.

"Out of everyone in my high school," Noll says today, thinking back to 1952 in Manhattan Beach, California, "just three of us were surfers. So of course we wanted to stand out. And right about then people were beginning to look at surfers as something different, and maybe a little

While Hollywood made "beach movies" for national distribution, surfers themselves made "surf films," which were shown in Kiwanis Club halls and high school auditoriums up and down the West Coast. Filmmaker Bruce Brown (below) holds up a handbill for his latest movie Waterlogged. Brown, at this point, was editing footage for his classic surf film, The Endless Summer.

The longboard revival began in the early 1980s, then exploded in the early 1990s. Half of all surfboards made today are over 9 feet long. "It comes down to glide, pure and simple," says Scott Hulet, editor of Longboard magazine. "Just two or three easy strokes to get into a wave. You're at hull speed right away. Then move up to the sweet spot and feel your way into trim. There's a kind of resonance there, as opposed to shortboard surfing, where a lot of times it's just turn, turn, turn until your board sinks." Longboard surfer Jeff Kramer, shown here, often maneuvers himself into what most would consider to be shortboard territory.

weird. I remember the vice-principal called me to his office, sat me down, and said, 'What exactly do you guys do down there on the beach?' He understood about the wave-riding part, but not the rest of it. We had 'em a little worried. And so we made a game of it. That was the beginning of what I guess you'd call the lifestyle."

The surfing culture has never been particularly hospitable to those women and girls who actually venture off the beach and into the waves. While their numbers are greater than ever before, just 15 percent of all surfers in America are female. California's Joyce Hoffman (below) was a stand-out surfer in the mid-1960s. (Opposite page) Taking a more aggressive route is Hawaii's Rochelle Ballard.

What exactly *are* they doing down there on the beach? Greg Noll's vice-principal, responding in the timeless manner of nonsurfers, wasn't so much interested in surfing itself as the effects of surfing—the ripples and reverberations, known collectively as "surf culture," that would soon move from the beaches into recording studios, movie theaters, fashion houses, and advertising agencies. The steady growth in surfing's popularity—from 100,000 active surfers internationally in the mid-1960s to perhaps 3 or 4 million today—offers little explanation as to how a coastal subculture could flap its wings and send a tornado across the fields of art, commerce, and the public imagination. And if surf culture will never again be as fresh and exciting as it was during Greg Noll's era, it has nonetheless been surprisingly resilient and adaptable through the years. A surf culture inventory today might begin with the thousands of warehouses full of surf-logo T-shirts and finish with the current wave—Noll must shudder at the thought—of "serious" surf literature.

Because nonsurfers have been vigorous and effective purveyors of surf culture for nearly 40 years, it's often hard to distinguish between the genuine surf article and forgeries. The public at large, for example, views the Beach Boys as a three-word definition of "surf music" and assumes that the band's members and core supporters were rank-and-file Southern California surfers. Wrong on all counts. Surf music, precisely defined, is instrumental-only, and features a sliding, heavy-reverb, jack-hammer guitar sound, along with a strong emphasis on the first beat of each measure. Perfection in the genre was reached with Dick Dale's 1962 hit "Miserlou"—later used for the opening credits in *Pulp Fiction*. Dale's shows at the Rendezvous Ballroom in Newport Beach in the early 1960s were heavily attended by surfers, and Dale himself was a passable surfer. The Beach Boys were another story. When the Hawthorne, California–based vocal group released its first

album, *Surfin' USA*, in 1963, trendsetters on the beach put them down not just as musically soft but as rip-off artists. Only the drummer surfed, and he was a kook; and Hawthorne, of course, was miles east of the Pacific Coast Highway. "Big in the Midwest, big in Japan . . . not big at Malibu," commented 1960s surf icon Lance Carson, a longtime R & B purist. But musical purity, in some cases, became harder to define with the passing years. "I really didn't like the Beach Boys at the time; none of us did," says *Surfer* founder John Severson. "But now when I hear those old songs, it brings back great memories of good waves and good times. So maybe it is surf music after all."

And now for something really different: California surfers Bobby Friedman and Ana Schisler ride tandem at the Pipeline. Debate would follow as to whether the act was progressive, absurd, or romantic. Friedman: "I couldn't believe how steep that wave was. We just dropped straight down." Schisler: "I just started paddling, and when I felt nothing but air, I figured it was time to stand up." They rode this wave successfully.

While the California beach sound that had much of the free world swaying and stomping in the early 1960s was an all-male invention, it was actually a teenage girl who stood at the headwaters of surfing culture. Kathy Kohner, 16, just a shade over 5 feet tall, went to Malibu in the summer of 1956 to learn how to surf, and was immediately given the nickname "Gidget"—a contraction of "girl midget." Two years later she enrolled in college and quit surfing forever, but the book *Gidget*, a milk-and-sugar version of Kathy's experiences on the beach, written by her father, Fritz, had by that time become a best-seller.

Fritz chose the right location. Malibu was then the fertile crescent of surf culture. Although the origins of wave-riding are traced back to ancient times, and the public had taken occasional notice of surfers throughout the first half of the 20th century, the sport's basic and lasting character was for the most part created at Malibu after World War II. James Dean, Marlon Brando, the Beat poets, and rock and roll did the essential nonconformist spade-work. Then surfers joined in, minus the brooding teenage angst, but often showing real proficiency in outraging the squares. To keep warm on the beach during cold mornings, surfers bought women's full-length fur coats for next-to-nothing at the Salvation Army. They wore peroxide-white hair as a badge. They bought $25 cars, splashed the exteriors with colored resin, then knocked out the rear windows for easier surfboard transportation. A well-known Malibu surfer, posing as Washington crossing the Delaware, once rode through a Winchell's parking lot on the hood of a friend's car, wearing a single, logically placed glazed donut.

Meanwhile, a code of surfing attitudes and mores, elitist beyond measure, was developed. Style and appearance ranked higher than money and privilege. Because Hawaii was revered as the sport's spiritual home, surfers garnished their lives with palm-frond hats, tiki gods, and bowls of pineapple-rum punch. Beginning surfers were publicly humiliated. "Gidget" would eventually find a small niche in women's studies courses as an Eisenhower-era feminist, but the sport's overwhelming maleness ensured that women would be treated badly. "Women were props, nothing else," recalls former big-wave surfer Fred Van Dyke. "You took the best-looking woman you could find, she'd sit on the beach all day, get sunburned and dehydrated, and the guy would come in and get pissed off because she didn't see his best ride. It was machismo to the nth degree."

"Malibu Lizards," a short fiction piece found in the 1960 debut edition of *Surfer Magazine*, hinted at surf-related adventures in travel, drinking, and sex, and few of the approximately 60 surf magazines that exist today have moved beyond this basic publishing philosophy. But the first *Surfer* also contained a postscript that articulated perfectly and for all time the solemn, metasport nature of surfing: "In this crowded world the surfer can still seek and find the perfect day, the perfect wave, and be alone with the surf and his thoughts."

Malibu was often the star attraction in the homespun surf films that annually toured the beach city community centers and high school auditoriums in the late 1950s and 1960s. The movies

Surfers in the late 1950s and early 1960s went all-out to create a distinctly new identity, and this included their choice of automobiles. While in high school, California surfer Mike Doyle paid $400 for a Cadillac hearse, which he painted canary yellow. Like any other teenager, he greatly enjoyed upsetting adults. But it went beyond that. "We had our own style now," Doyle wrote, years later. "We didn't have to act like square football jocks. The creative freedom and exhilaration we'd found in surfing was affecting our whole lives."

(early favorites included *Cat on a Hot Foam Board*, *The Angry Sea*, and *Waterlogged*) were formulaic: 75 minutes of whip-turns, nose-rides, big waves, and wipeouts, with a half-dozen short comedy sketches spliced in at regular intervals for a change of pace, all set to a tape-recorded rock-and-roll or jazz soundtrack. The howling audience reaction, especially during the opening few shots, was only partly related to what was being shown onscreen. The surf movie was a fuse. The real event was the crowd itself. In coastal town theaters, surfing identity was expressed in a single, ear-splitting voice, and people who were there still remember such moments as the greatest communal experience of their lives.

Before the *Gidget* travel sequels (first set in Hawaii, then Rome), and long before the *Gidget* TV series appeared, Kathy Kohner, in 1959, sat back in a theater with her Malibu friends Moondoggie and Tubesteak and watched the original *Gidget* movie. Hollywood would do a lot worse by surfing in years to come with *Beach Blanket Bingo*, *Beach Party*, and the other Annette Funicello/Frankie Avalon movies. At least *Gidget*, if only for dramatic tension, touched on the attraction of a life spent surfing. "Kahuna," the main surfing character in the movie, is played by Cliff Robertson and patterned after Terry "Tubesteak" Tracy—who lived for three summers in a shack on the point at Malibu. Kahuna is older than Gidget and the rest of the surfers in the movie. He's a serious surfer, and Robertson, looking great in a work shirt with torn-off sleeves, gives his character's defining line a serious reading: "I'm a surf bum. You know, ride the waves, eat, sleep, not a care in the world." Columbia scriptwriters allowed this independent notion to roam free for about 60 minutes before letting slip the dogs of American free enterprise. Kahuna gives up almost without struggle. In the movie's final scene, he tears down his beach shack, walks off the beach, and rejoins the work force.

The international success of Bruce Brown's *The Endless Summer*, in 1966 and 1967, was irrefutable proof that the mainstream could, under the right circumstances, pay attention to real surfing. Twenty years later, the sport again rode high on the wheel of trend, fashion, and a billion-dollar beach-clothing industry in the late 1980s. Then surfing hit a low period, followed by another high in the mid-1990s. By this time, wavepools and surf-theme nightclubs dotted the landscape. The professional surfing circuit could be seen weekly on TV. But surfing's material cultural output—its paraphernalia, gestures, and effects—would never again radiate off the beach the way they did in the early and mid-1960s. The surfer-as-sportsman makeover didn't take in the early and

Artifacts from surfing's past have in recent years become collectable. Balsa surfboards made in the 1950s sell for as much as $8,000. Early editions of Surfer Magazine can bring $500. These surf movie posters, which were hammered up by the thousands onto beach city telephone polls in the early 1960s, might sell for $100–$300 each.

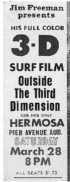
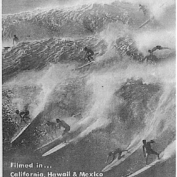

California surfer-designer Tom Morey hoped to bring surfing to the masses when he invented the "Morey Boogie" bodyboard in 1971, working with a slab of packing foam and an electric carving knife. He succeeded. 600,000 bodyboards are sold each year in America, compared to 125,000 surfboards. Easy use is the main reason. A stand-up surfer generally needs a year or more to acquire a rudimentary level of skill; a bodyboarder might gain competency in a single weekend. Meanwhile, the expert bodyboarder can make fantastic sport out of waves that aren't suited for stand-up surfing.

mid-1980s; urban street influences were picked up and discarded in the mid-1990s. These surfing personas ignored the lessons of *The Endless Summer*. Brown's film was warm, easy-going, iconoclastic, and soulful to the core. Genuine forms of surf culture almost always are.

Today, surf culture often seems to be little more than 1950s- and 1960s-based nostalgia. Surf memorabilia is collected, traded, and sold. Classic surf movies have been released on video. Reconstructed Woodies sell for $50,000 and longboards, nearly extinct in the 1970s, now account for half of all surfboard sales.

But new ground is being broken as well, as surfing for the first time is examined—by insiders and outsiders—in a more considered way. Beach volleyball is the new symbolic activity for the young, blonde, and dumb, lifting much of the burden from surfing. Most of what is new in surf culture today has to do with measuring the sport's significance. PBS in 1995 aired a 1-hour documentary called *Liquid Stage: The Lure of Surfing*. Art galleries and universities have staged surfing exhibits, and more than a dozen permanent surfing museums have opened up internationally in the past decade. Rhino Records has issued a four-CD compendium of surf music. A 12-part cable TV series, titled *Fifty Years of Surfing on Film*, aired in the summer of 1996. In 1997 a documentary on surfing and healthy aging is due to air, and Kem Nunn's surfing novel, *The Dogs of Winter*, will be published. Surfing, in other words, is currently being granted a weight and standing unimaginable during the era of Frankie and Annette.

Larger cultural shifts have also lent new status to the sport. Surfing fits nicely into a proenvironmental context. The Internet is constantly (if metaphorically) being "surfed." Flex time and telecommuting are ideal for a life strongly influenced by the cryptic forces of wind, tide, and ocean swell.

Finally, the image of the surfer—and, by association, surfing itself—is being recast. Daniel Duane's 1996 memoir, titled *Caught Inside: A Surfer's Year on the California Coast*, offered the longest and most thoughtful look yet at surfing's still-evolving place in society. Duane, throughout the book, talks with great admiration about his surfing mentor. "Vince was already running—not jogging, but outright sprinting—down the dirt road. Age 45, clean khakis and sun cap, board under one arm, pack on his back, bounding through the fields on a Monday. He surfed every day without fail, and often surfed twice a day. I loved being with him, loved our endless conversations and the unshakable sense that this unlikely use of time mattered."

It turns out that Vince is married and has a teaching job at a nearby college, but he nonetheless sounds very much like . . . a surf bum. Vince as Kahuna, based on Tubesteak: life imitating bad art imitating life.

Ride the waves, eat, sleep, not a care in the world. Surfers once had to grow out of surfing. Now they can grow into it. ♪

Better surfing through science? Skeptic Kelly Slater closely examines the stationary wave at the Schlitterhahn Water Park in Texas in 1994. Artificial surf has been a live issue for surfers over the past 3 decades. Hundreds of mechanical surf models have been designed, proposed, and, in a few dozen cases, built. Some surfers are thrilled by the notion of plentiful and predictable waves. Others are repelled, believing the organic field to be surfing's greatest attraction. (Opposite page) Rob Machado in Southern California.

While surf culture for the most part seems to exist in an atmosphere that is loud, fast-paced, and trendy, surfers themselves come to depend on the sport for long moments of calm.

ACKNOWLEDGMENTS

The author would like to thank the following people for their assistance, suggestions, and comments: Greg Ambrose, Meg Bernardo, Daniel Duane, Mark Fragale, Sam George, Sandra Hall, Steve Hawk, Scott Hulet, Bruce Jenkins, Brock Little, Mickey Muñoz, Ira Opper, Dori Payne, Steve Pezman, Mark Renneker, and Shaun Tomson. And special thanks to Michael Warshaw and Nancy Tompkins for reading the rough drafts.

SELECTED SOURCES

CHAPTER ONE: MORNING AT FRESHWATER

Hall, Sandra Kimberly, with Greg Ambrose. *Memories of Duke*. Honolulu: Bell Press, 1995.

Brennan, Joseph. *Duke: The Life Story of Duke Kahanamoku*. Honolulu: Ku Pa'a Publishing Inc., 1994.

Finney, Ben, and James Houston. *Surfing: A History of the Ancient Hawaiian Sport*. San Francisco: Pomegranate Artbooks, 1966.

Ball, John. *California Surfriders*. Los Angeles: Mountain & Sea Books, 2nd Edition, 1979.

Blake, Tom. *Hawaiian Surfriders*. Los Angeles: Mountain & Sea Books, 2nd Edition, 1983.

Severson, John. "The Duke: Interview with Duke Kahanamoku." *Surfer* (March 1965): 16-20.

Zurick, David. "Surfing Among the Ancient Hawaiians." *Surfer* (August 1987): 58-61.

Lynch, Gary. "Tom Blake: Beyond the Horizon." *Surfer* (November 1989): 74-80.

Young, Nat. *The History of Australian Surfing*. Nat Young Holdings and Yoho Productions, 1985. Video.

CHAPTER TWO: SURFARI

Lueras, Leonard. *Surfing: The Ultimate Pleasure*. New York: Workman Publishing, 1984.

Brown, Bruce. "Africa: the Perfect 'Cloud Nine.'" *Surfer* (March 1993): 42-51.

Hulet, Scott. "In Trim: Mike Hynson." *Longboard* (Winter 1992): 26-35.

"Surfers and Beasts." *The New Yorker* (July 9, 1966): 78.

"Surf's Up." *Time* (July 8, 1966): 84.

"Ten at the Top." *Newsweek* (January 9, 1967): 63.

Dora, Mickey. "Mickey on Malibu." *Surfer* (January 1968): 37-42.

Fifty Years of Surfing on Film. Opper Sports, 1996. Video.

The Endless Summer. Bruce Brown Films, 1964. Film.

The Search. High Voltage/Rip Curl Wetsuits, 1992. Video.

CHAPTER THREE: THE HEAT OF COMPETITION

George, Matt. "The Art and Soul of Rob Machado," *Surfing* (June 1996): 100-107.

Marcus, Ben. "Ascent of the Thin Man," *Surfer* (March 1994): 54-57.

Warshaw, Matt. "Masterpiece Theater: The Pipeline Masters Turns 25." *The Surfer's Journal* (Winter 1995): 78-95.

"Win, Place, Show." *Surfer* (February 1996): 106.

Barilotti, Steve. "Master of His Destiny." *Surfer* (April 1995): 104-112.

Walker, Matt. "3-Peat!" *Eastern Surf Magazine* (February 1996): 50-54.

What!? Kozo Productions, 1994. Video.

CHAPTER FOUR: REVOLUTION

St. Pierre, Brian. *The Fantastic Plastic Voyage*. New York: Coward-McCann, 1969.

Young, Nat. *The History of Surfing*. Palm Beach, Australia: Palm Beach Press, 1983.

Farrelly, Midget. *The Surfing Life*. New York: Arco Publishing Co., 1967.

McTavish, Bob, with Nat Young and John Witzig. "Three Views of the Revolution." *The Surfer's Journal* (Fall 1995): 40-67.

Kampion, Drew. "The Super Short, Uptight, V-Bottom, Tube-Carving, Plastic Machines." *Surfer* (September 1968): 40-48.

Witzig, John. "The Challenge from Down Under." *Surfer* (July 1968): 84-92.

McNulty, Patrick. "The Duke Does It Again." *Surfer* (March 1968): 30-35.

George, Sam. "The Evolution of Soul: How Surfboards Got from There to Here." *Surfer* (April 1996): 90-95.

"Hemmings Is Hot! An Interview with Fred Hemmings." *Surfer* (November 1968): 66-69.

Duclos, Jeff. "In Trim: Dewey Weber." *Longboard* (September 1996): 35-43.

Witzig, John, with Bob McTavish and Nat Young. "A New Era," "An End to an Era?" and "1966 Australian Championships." *Surfing World* (July 1966).

The Hot Generation. Produced by Paul Witzig, 1968. Film.

Young, Nat. *The History of Australian Surfing*. Nat Young Holdings and Yoho Productions, 1985. Video.

CHAPTER FIVE: THE UNRIDDEN REALM

Johnson, Pete. "Gunmen." *Surfing* (June 1996): 30-42.

George, Matt. "In God's Hands." *Surfing* (June 1996): 44-48.

Slater, Evan. "Expanding the Unridden Realm." *Surfer* (October 1996): 200-201.

George, Sam. "In the Land of the Giants." *Surfer* (July 1996): 104-111.

Little, Brock. "Pressure Drop." *Surfer* (May 1990): 118-124.

Carroll, Nick. "Thanksgiving." *Surfing* (April 96): 86-95.

McMahon, Bucky. "The Hydrophonic Dreams of Laird Hamilton." *Outside* (June 1994): 76-84.

Lopez, Gerry. "Quantum Leap: Jet Assisted Take Off." *The Surfer's Journal* (Spring 1995): 82-103.

"Full Throttle." *Surfer* (June 1995): 62-67.

Marcus, Ben. "Power Surfing: The Next Realm: Take II." *Surfer* (September 1994): 52-61.

Jenkins, Bruce. "The Next Realm?" *Surfer* (December 1993): 48-55.

Beyond Monster Maverick's. Magalodon Productions, 1996. Video.

Endless Summer II. New Line Productions, 1994. Film.

Surf Crazy. Bruce Brown Films, 1960. Film.

CHAPTER SIX: SURFORAMA

Severson, John. *Modern Surfing Around the World.* New York: Doubleday & Co., 1964.

Duane, Daniel. *Caught Inside: A Surfer's Year on the California Coast.* New York: North Point Press, 1996.

Noll, Greg, and Andrea Gabbard. *Da Bull: Life Over the Edge.* Berkeley: North Atlantic Books, 1989.

Doyle, Mike, with Steve Sorensen,. *Morning Glass: The Adventures of Legendary Waterman Mike Doyle.* Three Rivers, California: Manzanita Press, 1993.

Surf Guide. Assorted ads and articles. (December 1963 and March 1964).

"Surf-O-Rama." *The Surfer's Journal* (Winter 1994): 98-99.

"Surfing Goes Hollywood." *Surf Guide* (March 1964): 28-31.

"The Surf Fad." *Surf Guide* (October 1963): 19.

Warshaw, Matt. "When Malibu Ruled." *Los Angeles Times* (May 1994): 48-55.

The Surfer. (Premier issue, 1960).

Heart, Jack. "Standing in Line for the Last Surfing Movie." *Surfer* (April 1975): 84-90.

Barilotti, Steve. "Jazz Man: Tom Morey—the Man Who Gave Waves to the World." *Surfer* (February 1996): 98-103.

Fifty Years of Surfing on Film. Opper Sports, 1996. Video.

Gidget. Columbia Pictures, 1959. Film.

Ride the Wild Surf. Columbia Pictures, 1964. Film.

The Endless Summer. Bruce Brown Films, 1964. Film.

Cowabunga: The Surf Box. Rhino Records, 1996. CD box set.

PHOTOGRAPHY CREDITS

Erik Aeder: 1, 38, 43, 110-111a-e, 122.

Kirk Aeder: 63j, 66.

Don Balch: 89, 128-129.

Bob Barbour: 105.

Brian Bielmann: 52-53.

John Bilderback: 57a, 57b.

Bishop Museum: 16-17, 18b, 19, 20, 21 (Tai Sing Loo), 22, 27, 28a, 28b (A.R. Gurley, Jr.), 29 (Howard Livingston Hill), 30, 31.

Bruce Brown: 34b, 35, 49.

Robert Brown: 4-5.

Bud Browne: 94b.

John Callahan: 42a, 42b, 42c, 46, 47, 48, 51, 70-71a-o, 132.

Sylvain Cazenave: 12, 87d, 91, 106-107, 108, 109.

Jeff Divine: 6, 39, 45, 67, 81, 85, 86b, 90, 100-101, 102, 121, 127.

Rick Doyle: 2-3, 10, 11, 13, 15, 18a, 34a, 54a, 55a, 55b, 55c, 55d, 55e, 55f, 55g, 55h, 65, 74a, 88, 94a, 114a, 125, 126.

Rob Gilley: 44, 50, 59, 60-61, 62-63, 82, 103, 104.

Ted Grambeau: 36, 40-41.

Leroy Grannis: 23, 24, 25, 62a, 62b, 62c, 62e, 62f, 62i, 62j, 62m, 62n, 76, 77, 78, 79, 115, 116, 117, 120, 123.

Dr. Don James: 26a, 26b, 95, 97, 112-113.

Craig Peterson: 37.

Jim Russi: 32-33, 55i, 55j, 55k, 58, 63h, 64, 69, 83, 99, 118-119.

Tom Servais: 8-9, 54b, 57c, 62d, 62h, 62k, 62l, 62o, 62p, 63a, 63b, 63c, 63d, 63e, 63f, 63g, 63i, 63k, 63l, 63m, 68, 72-73, 84, 86a, 86c, 86d, 87a, 87b, 87c.

Surfer Magazine: 62g.

Steve Wilkings: 80, 96, 114b, 124a, 124b, 124c, 124d.

Scott Winer: 98.

John Witzig: 74b, 75.

Darrell Wong: 92-93.